THE
WICCA
HANDBOOK

THE WICCA HANDBOOK

A COMPLETE GUIDE
TO WITCHCRAFT & MAGIC

SHEENA MORGAN

vega

Acknowledgements

First I'd like to thank Vivianne and Chris for introducing me to the Craft of the Wise and for their unfailing kindness, support and generosity. Love and thanks too to my High Priest Mike and especially to my High Priestess Laura for their impeccable attitude to magic and for all their love and care. Next I have to say a huge thank you to Neil Sutherland and Steve Morley for their fantastic photographs and for regularly putting in 15-hour days to get the right shot and to our stunning models Mike and Agni, Michael and Inbaal, Michelle, Max, Mark and Lee, who all worked so hard.

I'm also indebted to all of the priests and priestesses including Harry, Sandy, Mike, Marie, Litsa, Judith, Gillian and Laura who shared their thoughts on Wicca.

Finally and most importantly thanks to Jane Alexander for organizing the whole project and to David and Indi for allowing us to take over their home so often while the book was coming together. Thanks everyone and Blessed Be.

The publishers would like to thank NinyaMikhaila.com, historical costumier; Robert Kennedy of the Wand Workshop (info@wandworkshop.co.uk) for the kind loan of his crystal wands; Cobra Whips for the loan of their scourges; Wool of Bat for the loan of robes; the Wyrdshop for the loan of a Cernunnos statue; and Penny Murphy and Sarah Davis for their generous assistance.

© Vega 2003
Text © Sheena Morgan 2003

ISBN 1-84333-697-9

A catalogue record for this book is available from the British Library

A member of **Chrysalis** Books plc

First published in 2003 by
Vega
64 Brewery Road
London, N7 9NT

Visit our website at
www.chrysalisbooks.co.uk

Printed and bound in Hong Kong

Design and retouching: Mark Buckingham
Project management: Jane Alexander
Photography: Neil Sutherland, Steve Morley
Production: Susan Sutterby

Contents

Chapter 1
UNDERSTANDING WICCA

THE GIFT OF THE GODS

Call me old-fashioned, but when I hear the word 'witchcraft' I get a little thrill of excitement. It's the associations – the broomsticks, cauldrons, magic spells and midnight rites with witches dancing naked round bonfires under moonlit skies.

Today, witchcraft still contains all of these things, but what surprises many people is that witchcraft also offers much more. In addition to practical magic, witchcraft offers its practitioners a deep sense of being in harmony with the yearly cycle of the seasons, a feeling of community with all forms of life on the planet and a profound sense of the mystery involved in the worship of the divine in all things. I count myself very lucky to be a witch and consider it a great honour to have been initiated into the Craft of the Wise.

Of course, sceptics are quick to point out that contemporary witchcraft, or Wicca, is a revival, not a survival, of an ancient pagan tradition – a modern construct put together in the middle of the last century by Gerald Gardner and his High Priestess, Doreen Valiente. In one sense, they are right. Modern Wicca has evolved fairly recently and many of the rites of most Gardnerian covens may be no more than 50 years old. How, then, can witches claim to be exponents of 'the old religion' and expect to be taken seriously? In answer, most witches would point out that a belief in our ability to connect with the unseen forces of the universe, the honouring of masculine and feminine archetypes and the celebration of a yearly

seasonal cycle have been undertaken, continuously, all over the world for many thousands of years. Wicca is part of this greater tradition.

WICCA TODAY

Wicca offers its followers a chance to establish their own place in relation to the tides of energy that connect us with the great web of existence; it forms an adaptable system of beliefs, revolving around an acknowledgement of the divine in nature. Wiccans believe that all life is sacred, so they aim to conserve and protect the earth and all her life forms.

Wicca is also a 'mystery religion'. Its practitioners undertake three levels of initiation, known as the First, Second and Third Degrees. Initiates join a priesthood and are empowered to create their own rituals. Wicca encourages self-examination and, by providing a flexible but supportive framework, it allows individuals to embark on a life-long voyage of spiritual self-discovery and development.

Last, but most important of all, Wicca offers direct and personal contact with the numinous, or sacred. In Wiccan rituals, everyone plays an equal role in creating sacred space and worshipping the Gods.

While witches believe in one supernal, creative web, they honour the life force as a polarity and worship a Goddess and a God, based on a tradition that is possibly prehistoric. In Europe, carved figures have been found that represent, in a rudimentary but powerful way, ancient symbols of a matriarch, or 'Great Mother'. Later, this creatrix is joined, in cave paintings, by a horned male figure – a blend of man and beast, now called the 'The Horned One'.

'Some call me Jack, or Pan, or Puck
By many names men do me know
But in the forest and the glade
Men call me Robin Goodfellow.

Robin in the Hood, Robin of the Wood
Through dark and moonlit nights I go,
My queen, May Marion, at my side
Dancing ever to and fro.'

The Practice of Wicca

Wiccans worship a Goddess as well as a God. This makes them pretty unusual in the Western world. Most Western spiritual paths are based on a masculine, paternal godhead and leave no room for the divine feminine. Yet it seems that our need to acknowledge the polarity of our existence will always reassert itself. Even in Christianity, the Goddess appears, albeit in a rather curtailed form, as Mary, mother of Christ – revered, but not divine.

THE TRIPLE GODDESS

In Wicca the Goddess, the sacred aspect of the female, is given her rightful place and accorded all due honour. Often called 'The Great Mother' or 'The Triple Goddess', she is believed to be the primordial creatrix, whose boundless tides of matter and energy brought the first life into being. The Goddess is worshipped in three forms: as the Maiden, eternally young, virginal and ever-renewing; as the Mother, a mature sensual and sexual being who brings both love and pain; and as the Crone of Wisdom, who presides over the mysteries of the grave. The Goddess allows us to see different aspects of herself during the yearly cycle, yet her true nature does not change. This seeming contradiction is the essence of her being – constant and enduring, ever changing yet never changing.

The moon is the Wiccan symbol of the Goddess and its waxing, full and waning phases correspond to her three faces. However, while Wiccans revere the moon as a symbol of the Goddess, they do not worship the moon, nor do they worship the sun, symbol of the God.

KNOWING THE GOD

The God is the eternal son, lover and companion of the Goddess. Like her, he has several aspects and these correspond to his traditional duties as both a hunting and an agricultural deity. In the older of the two

Above
A woodland altar dedicated to Robin Goodfellow, the Lord of the green wood.

roles, as the Horned God, his symbolic antlers signal that he is divine and mark him out as both the hunter and the prey. As the sacrificial 'Lord of the Hunt', he guards the the gateway between our realm and the mysteries of the underworld.

The God's other aspect is that of a solar/ vegetation/fertility spirit. As he grows in strength, comes to maturity and impregnates the Goddess, so the sun moves from its weakest point at the midwinter solstice to its zenith at midsummer. The God ensures the fertility of the Goddess and, in consequence, the abundance of the coming harvest. To achieve this, he sacrifices himself as the Corn King and allows his blood to spill onto the earth. With the God's sacrifice comes the waning of the year, when the sun's power begins to falter. At this point the God retreats below the ground to become the Lord of the Underworld. A new God is born at the midwinter solstice and the fertility of the Goddess is once again assured. This cycle reinforces the belief that, while a new God must sacrifice himself every year to maintain the fertility of the Goddess and the land, the Goddess herself, the life force of the universe, never dies.

WICCAN TRADITIONS

There are many Wiccan traditions, among them Gardnerian, Alexandrian and Dianic, but the basic pattern is the same whichever tradition you follow. There is a fundamental framework of festivals, or Sabbats, which are tied to the seasons and held throughout the year. These are Samhain, Yule, Imbolc, the Vernal Equinox, Beltane, Summer Solstice, Lammas and the Autumn Equinox. Esbats also take place every full moon. At all these rituals a magic circle is created, within which the rites take place. While sabbat rites primarily acknowledge and celebrate the Gods and the changing seasons, esbats tend to be used for the practical making of magic.

Wiccan Beliefs

Witches are an anarchistic lot. If you asked a hundred witches to describe what they believe, you would probably come up with a hundred different answers. This is as it should be. Witchcraft does not subscribe to dogmas or to 'received teachings' from gurus. It is a religious path that is constantly evolving and which is not based on any one fixed text. While Gardnerian and Alexandrian Wiccans still copy out Gardner's Book of Shadows by hand, the rituals within it are seen as more of a starting point. They are the basis for creating one's own rites, rather than some sort of manual to be slavishly followed.

However, although witches are independently minded, there are several commonly held strands of belief that colour everything witches do. First and foremost, witches believe that each person, animal, rock, fish, tree, insect, bird

Above
Greeting a new dawn reaffirms every Wiccan's connection to the elements and to all forms of life.

Right
A priestess uses a ritual sword to cast a circle, creating a 'space between the worlds'.

or plant is part of the one great life force, which animates the universe. All are interconnected and all are imbued with divinity.

As most of the natural world procreates using a two-gender system, witches honour the life force as both male and female. Doreen Valiente (one of the founders of modern Wicca) describes the energy arising out of this sexual polarity as 'creative tension' and claims it is this energy that witches use to fuel their magical work.

WICCA AND MAGIC

All witches believe in magic, or the ability to affect their world through psychic means. If they didn't believe in magic, they wouldn't be witches. Witches view the universe as a multitude of seen and unseen strata – they understand the power of the natural world and accept all of its levels, known and unknown, as natural, rather than 'supernatural' or 'paranormal'.

These adjoining and interconnected worlds are thought to have far-reaching effects on each other and can encompass the physical, spiritual and mental spheres. Through techniques like meditation and trance, practitioners of magic learn how to gain access to more than one realm.

Some physicists are currently putting forward the theory that such 'other worlds' exist physically in a domain they describe as 'dark matter' – that over 90 per cent of the cosmos is made up of 'dark matter', and the universe we experience is suspended in, supported and penetrated by these particles. If this is true, it does not seem so far-fetched for witches to claim that their magical work, which is intended to operate on more than one level, should have a tangible effect on their everyday world.

Finally, all witches share the belief that the soul is eternal. Some believe in the idea that the soul returns to earth time after time, constantly expanding its spiritual knowledge and exploring the nature of what it means to be human. Others believe that our bodies return to the earth to be transformed into the new life of plants and animals, while our souls become universal and eternal energy. Whatever their individual beliefs, all witches share a common conviction that the soul continues after physical death.

What Wicca is not

Even today, many people still have lots of misconceptions about what Wicca and witchcraft actually entail. People regularly seem to confuse witchcraft with Satanism or devil worship and to imagine that, because many Wiccans work 'skyclad' (in a state of ritual nudity), Wiccan rites are little more than orgies. Sometimes it is just as important to state what Wicca is not, as to tell people what it is.

Wicca is a mystery religion that does not seek new adherents. Wiccans are more than happy to accept that other religions are equally valid and that there are many different routes to the same end. Because of this, Wiccans do not proselytize or try to convert those of other religions. The truth is that covens very rarely have to seek out new members. In fact the reverse is true; most covens have waiting lists of people who are eager to learn the Craft of the Wise. Every Wiccan presently working in a coven will have had to try long and persistently to find their current homes.

WITCHES ARE NOT SATANISTS

Witches don't worship Satan. Satan is a Christian concept – a spirit, representing evil, that Christians believe to be the adversary of their God Jehovah. Satanists are Christians who have rebelled against the teachings of their own Church.

Traditionally Satanists perform the 'Black Mass', which is carried out by a defrocked priest. This rite is a blasphemous parody of the Catholic sacrament in which the crucifix is suspended upside down and animals may be ritually slaughtered.

WITCHES ARE NOT DEVIL WORSHIPPERS

It's true that Wiccans worship a horned male deity who is known as the Horned One, but he is by no means a figure of evil. His horns are ancient symbols of divinity and authority. These symbolic horns have been shared by, among others, Alexander the Great and the prophet Moses. As Cernunnos, Lord of the Hunt, the God bears the sacred antlers of the stag. He presides over the hunt and guards us on our passage from life, through the portal of death to the Underworld. In the green of the year, the Horned One is often represented as the goat-footed and goat-horned Pan, the spirit of sexual pursuit – lust-filled, virile and life-affirming.

When Britain was a pagan country, the Horned God was worshipped everywhere. Such was his importance that, when Christianity was introduced – in the 6th century – the early Church fathers were at great pains to curtail his power. It is often said that the Gods of an earlier religion become the devils of the later one, and this was certainly true in the case of the Horned God. Although the Christian Church adapted and adopted some pagan symbolism, it found the Horned God's open sexuality unacceptable and, over the years, his name was linked with that of Satan. His horns and cloven hooves, originally symbols of his sanctity and affinity with nature, became corrupted into attributes of the Christian Devil.

However, such was the power of the Horned God that, despite all attempts to destroy him, he continued to appear in almost every place of Christian worship, from village church to cathedral, during the Middle Ages and beyond. His horns transformed into leaves and with stems and branches thrusting from his mouth (in what some claim is an ancient phallic gesture), the Horned One, or Green Man, is still a decorative presence in many Christian churches to this day. In spite of the centuries-long slur on his true nature, the Horned God remains a deity of strength, optimism and protection.

Right
Dressed in black, the colour of spirit, four witches dance to raise energy.

14

WICCAN RITUALS ARE NOT ORGIES

Many Wiccans work in a state of ritual nudity, commonly known as 'working skyclad'. Gerald Gardner stated that his initiators had insisted nudity was 'believed to be essential to facilitate the release of magical power'. While much argument still takes place about the veracity of this idea, ritual nudity does have one very useful magical purpose. It helps witches recognize themselves as they really are. In our ordinary lives it is easy to erect barriers and to hide behind masks.

Our society encourages us to define ourselves by what we do, rather than who we are. Working 'skyclad' erases those barriers. Ritual nudity frees witches from embarrassment and embarrassment is one of the great inhibitors of magical work.

Wiccans use the sexual energy or 'chemistry' between the male and female polarities to raise power during our rites. This does not mean that our rituals are excuses for illicit sexual activity – quite the reverse. Some covens will only operate with pairs of 'magical partners' who are

Below
Rocking the figure as if it were a child, a priestess blesses a healing poppet with a pentacle.

either married or are in a long-term relationship. Even if this is not the case, within a ritual circle the formal kiss of the priest or priestess conveys a blessing rather than any titillating sexual thrill.

SEX AND MAGIC

Of course Wiccans use ritual sex magic. Powerful emotions release powerful energy and what could be more effective than an orgasm to release magical intent into the universe? Witches feel there is nothing to be ashamed of in using this natural magical power.

However, almost all Wiccans would advocate that sex magic should be a private affair. The majority of Wiccans would never consider taking part in any form of sexual magic unless they were in a stable relationship with their magical partners.

If you are new to Wicca, be very wary of anyone who suggests that sexual intercourse is part of a First Degree initiation ritual. Never consider sex magic with anyone who is not your romantic partner of some standing and who is not of the same spiritual path as yourself. It doesn't matter how much of a free spirit you consider yourself to be – sex always leads to emotional involvement on some level, and this is particularly true when you combine sex and magic.

HEXING AND CURSING

Sadly, one of the most enduring images of witchcraft is of a witch stabbing a pin into a 'poppet' (a doll-like figure) representing a victim, in order to kill them. In fact modern Wicca advocates harmony and synthesis rather than antagonism, and poppets are used more often to heal than to hurt. One of the most important things you learn as a Wiccan is to think before you act and to ensure your actions cause no harm. Like other spiritual paths, Wicca has a code of ethics, which is often

encapsulated in a line from the 'Wiccan Rede' (a traditional verse, summing up the lore of witchcraft):

'An it harm none, do what you will.'

This means that you are free to do as you wish provided that your actions cause no harm to anything or anyone. This ethos has deep repercussions for how witches live day to day because witches see themselves as totally responsible for their actions.

On a spiritual level, the Wiccan Rede means the choices you make should be dictated by your will or higher self and should reflect your individual path of growth and development. When Wiccans make important decisions about their lives, these are based on a desire to fulfil their potential in accordance with their higher selves.

THREEFOLD RETURN

Some Wiccans also believe in the Law of Threefold Return. This states that whatever energy you send into the universe returns to you magnified three times. Therefore if you send out evil intent, you will suffer the same evil, only three times worse. Some believe this concept incorporates the idea of a kind of karmic scorecard in the sky and find it too close to the Christian idea of sin and retribution. Just as many Wiccans believe that, as a witch, you take responsibility for your actions and live with the consequences, good or bad.

While Wiccans are, in a way, 'self-policing', this does not mean that they allow themselves to be attacked or to become victims. They will act to prevent others from harming them or their families. Some witches use the power of reflection and bounce any negative energy back to the sender.

Above
A priest and priestess share a ritual kiss during a Beltane rite.

Why Choose Wicca?

KINSHIP WITH THE LAND

Gerald Gardner once said that witches are 'much closer to the soil' than those on other magical paths. Many are drawn to Wicca by a love of the earth and a desire to honour the land that supports us. In Wicca we see the earth as our creatrix, the womb from which we first sprang and the mother who now sustains us. More than any other Western tradition, Wicca ties its practitioners to the land, in a series of festivals that celebrate and mark the year's turning.

Right
A High Priest drums to summon the spirits of the woods.

Below
Traditionally placed on a Wiccan altar, the antlers of a stag reach skyward, symbolizing the power of Cernunnos.

WORSHIPPING THE GODS

The Wiccan Goddess and God symbolize the power that is in every man and every woman – the power to create life, to love, to protect that which we love and to find the courage to face death. Vivianne Crowley makes the point that Wiccans worship, not because they are compelled to out of fear, but because they love their Gods. In Wicca there is no pressure to worship, no strict rules of when and where to worship, no sense of sin or punishment if religious observance is not made. Many Wiccans simply worship their Gods because they feel an overwhelming sense of devotion and a desire to make personal contact with the divine.

INDIVIDUAL EXPERIENCES

Many of those who feel prompted to seek out Wicca do so because they have had otherworldly experiences either as children or as adults. These may include having psychic episodes, visions of other realms, encounters with deities or with mythological beings, or clear memories of a previous life. Some find it easy to assimilate these experiences. Others may repress them, or avoid exploring their meaning until later in life.

Some people simply 'feel' like witches. Frequently they find they are content in their own company. They may have had an interest in magic or the occult from an early age. They might enjoy a natural affinity with birds, animals or plants, be sensitive to changes in the weather, or have a gift for healing or clairvoyance.

THE CRAFT OF THE WISE

Some are drawn to Wicca not simply to connect with the Gods, but because they want to learn and to experience in a practical way the craft, or the making of magic. They may want to learn more about methods of divination, or about magical herbs and how these can be used in healing. They may seek knowledge of the magical uses of incense or how to create spells, potions and charms. Some may also want to learn how to weave and dye cloths for robes, how to carve wands and staffs, or how to make their own wine for use in rituals. Wicca offers all its initiates access to a huge store of traditional knowledge and skill.

ECSTASY

Finally there are those who seek out Wicca because they want to experience ecstasy, the sensation of being outside the body.

Wicca uses an established and accessible route that helps individuals achieve this sense of ecstatic release. Within the loose structure of its rituals, Wicca creates opportunities for incantation, drumming, chanting, trance and invocation (the calling down of deities into a priest or priestess). All of these methods aid the practitioner in leaving the body and attaining a sense of existing beyond the physical – of being at one with the cosmos.

A WORD OF WARNING

There are always some who are drawn to the practice of Wicca for the wrong reasons. There are many reasons for this – they may be seeking what they consider to be the glamour of 'forbidden' or 'occult' practices. They may be motivated by a desire to exert power over others or to find material wealth or notoriety. They may even be mistakenly seeking some kind of forlorn sexual thrill.

These souls will not thrive in Wicca unless they are prepared to change, for Wicca is a spiritual path that highlights, rather than indulges or glosses over, any personal shortcomings.

Our Wiccan Ancestors

Modern Wicca, be it Gardnerian, Alexandrian or Dianic, originally evolved from an eclectic mix of influences including freemasonry, ritual magic, theosophy, folklore, woodcraft and traditional witchcraft.

EARLY GARDNERIAN WICCA

In the late 1930s, when Gerald Gardner began searching for a coven to initiate him, hereditary or traditional covens were extremely secretive and usually recruited members exclusively from within family lines. There was, however, a strong 'ritual magic' infrastructure in Britain. From the freemasonry lodges of the late 19th century, master masons such as Wynn-Wescott, MacGregor-Mathers and W.J. Hughan created the Isis Urania lodge. This influential magical group was established

within The Hermetic Order of the Golden Dawn, the aim of which was a synthesis of Western magical traditions. Isis Urania drew on the philosophy of the Rosicrucians, on theosophy and, most strongly, on freemasonry. By the early 20th century, the lodge had among its members the poets W.B. Yeats and 'Fiona McLeod', A.E. Waite, the folklorist Lady Gregory and the magician Aleister Crowley.

Gerald Gardner was interested both in the Rosicrucians and in co-masonry (the branch that included women). In the late 1930s he joined the Rosicrucian theatre at Christchurch, in Hampshire, which had well-established links with co-masonry. It is said that through the theatre Gardner was introduced to Dorothy Clutterbuck, who, it is believed, initiated him into the Southern Coven of British Witches in 1939.

Below
A priestess connects with the energy of fire by casting an invoking pentacle during a midnight ritual.

There is still some uncertainty about whether Gardner was, in fact, initiated by Dorothy Clutterbuck. It seems likely that he worked with another High Priestess named Daffo during this period and her ritual format may have been adopted by Gardner. This same format is believed to be found in many modern Wiccan rituals. Gardner later claimed that the coven he had joined was a surviving remnant of the 'old religion' and that its practices had been handed down through generations.

PUBLICITY OR PRESERVATION

Almost immediately Gardner fell foul of his High Priestess as he wanted to make public the coven's rituals and practices. Whether he was prompted by a desire for self-publicity, or by a passionate belief that British witchcraft would not survive unless younger people were made aware of its existence, is not clear; but it is claimed the coven prevented him from publishing any of their rituals for the following ten years.

In the 1940s Gardner was introduced to Aleister Crowley by a mutual friend, Arnold Crowther. In 1946 Crowley made Gardner a member of the Ordo Templi Orientis, a German magical group with a heavy emphasis on tantric sex magic, freemasonry and nature lore.

In the late 1940s Gardner produced Ye Bok of Ye Art Magical, a precursor of his later magical work The Book of Shadows. Gardner claimed the work was an authentic ancient text. In fact he had put together a mixture of Crowley's original work, poetry by Rudyard Kipling, teachings from the Golden Dawn and snippets of ancient Sumerian invocations, along with his own coven's rites, all of which he presented in pseudo-archaic language. Despite Gardner's need to make his material appear antiquated by fakery, some of the material from Gardner's coven may have been authentically old.

In 1949 Gardner published the novel *High Magic's Aid* under his magical name, Scire. In it he reproduced many of the coven's rituals under the guise of fiction. He went on to explain the working of modern covens more fully in *Witchcraft Today*, in 1954. Gardner drew censure from the older members of his coven who believed that publicity could only harm traditional witchcraft.

In 1953 Gardner initiated Doreen Valiente, who went on to become his High Priestess and was responsible for rewriting much of The Book of Shadows. It annoyed Gardner immensely when Valiente pointed out that she recognized two of his supposedly archaic sources as Crowley and Kipling. Valiente removed much of Crowley's text, reworked many of the rituals in line with her own interest in Leland's *Gospel of the Witches* and rewrote the 'Charge of the Goddess'. The Charge, a poetic summary of the Wiccan ethos, is still regularly used in rites.

ALEXANDRIAN WICCA

Over the next ten years Gerald Gardner initiated, among others, Patricia Dawson, Eleanor (Rae) Bone, Lois Bourne and later Monique Wilson. Patricia Dawson married Gardner's old friend Arnold Crowther and went on to become a well-known writer and speaker on witchcraft.

One of the Crowthers' initiates, Pat Kopanski, initiated Alex Sanders in 1964, Sanders having earlier been refused initiation by the Crowthers. He married fellow coven member Maxine Morris and founded what was later dubbed Alexandrian Wicca. Sanders favoured a more ceremonial and slightly more complicated approach to rituals, some of which were robed. In 1970 the Sanders initiated Stewart Farrar, who, with the help of his wife Janet, wrote some of the definitive texts on Alexandrian Wicca – *Eight Sabbats for Witches*, *The Witches' Way* and *What Witches Do*.

Doreen Valiente worked with Gardner for several years and, despite their frequent differences over Gardner's 'publicity seeking', she remained very loyal to her initiator. Then, in the late 1950s, Gardner produced some new 'laws', claiming them to be of great antiquity. Valiente was sure these had been concocted by Gardner and coven member Jack Bracelin, with the purpose of replacing her in the coven. She believed that Gardner wished to make Monique Wilson his new High Priestess.

Valiente left Gardner's coven and, in 1964, began working with Ron Bowers (better known as Robert Cochrane) in the Clan of Tubal-Cain. Cochrane was openly critical of Gardnerian Wicca and evolved what he considered to be a more mystical and traditional approach. His covens were robed, and committed to working outside whenever possible. In the 1960s Cochrane began corresponding with the American Joe Wilson. Their letters formed the basis of the American Cochrane branch known as '1734'; one of its better-known covens was The Roebuck.

Valiente later parted company with Cochrane and spent many years working both as a solitary witch and with her magical partner. She wrote, among other books, *The ABC of Witchcraft, Witchcraft for Tomorrow* and *The Rebirth of Witchcraft*.

Gardner did indeed replace Valiente with Monique Wilson and he and Wilson worked together until his death. During that time, they initiated Raymond Buckland, who was partly responsible for popularizing Wicca in the United States.

In recent years, Gardnerian and Alexandrian covens in the States have become known as 'traditional' and make much of their lineage. In Britain, however,

Left
A skyclad High Priestess attunes herself to the energy of a standing stone.

'traditional' witchcraft is usually taken to mean hereditary witchcraft or country hedgewitchcraft.

WICCA IN THE USA

Other strands of witchcraft were also developing in America in the 1960s and 70s, among them the Faerie Wicca of Victor Anderson and the Dianic Wicca of Zsuzsanna Budapest, which aimed to combine feminist militancy and political activism. Budapest wrote the *Holy Book of Women's Mysteries,* and formed her first coven in the early 70s. One of her most well-known initiates is Miriam Simos, better known by her magical name Starhawk. Simos, who was also initiated into Faerie Wicca, went on to write one of America's most popular books on Wicca, *The Spiral Dance.*

On his death in 1964, Gerald Gardner bequeathed all his magical tools and the contents of his museum of witchcraft to Monique Wilson. For nine years she and her husband ran the witchcraft museum in the Isle of Mann, before selling off both the tools and the contents of the museum to Ripley's International, who staged sensational, carnival-like shows under the title 'Ripley's Believe It or Not'.

In Britain, in the 60s and 70s, Gardner's initiate Rae Bone initiated, among many others, a couple named Madge and Arthur. Their initiates included Prudence Jones, John and Caitlin Matthews and Vivianne Crowley, who was also initiated into Alexandrian Wicca by the Sanders. Many modern British covens embrace both Gardnerian and Alexandrian traditions.

Over the last fifty years, as new traditions continued to develop and grow, Wicca has thrived in Britain, Europe and Australia and seen a huge expansion as a feminist, spiritual path in the States. Whatever his true motivation, Gardner's publicizing of Wicca has ensured that the Craft of the Wise has not faded into obscurity.

Magic in the Modern World

It's hard to spot witches nowadays. Unless you live in Salem, Massachusetts, where it is almost de rigueur for American witches to sport cloaks and pointed hats, it's difficult to tell who is a witch and who isn't. If you encounter a gloomy, pale-faced soul, dressed in black velvet and drooping in some glum alcove, the chances are that he or she is not a witch. Witches have better things to do. Because witches love life and embrace it, they are much more likely to be at the centre of any social gathering than languishing dismally at the sidelines.

If Wiccans do have any obvious traits nowadays, then these are probably a sense of humour, self-awareness, determination to succeed in whatever they attempt to do, a strong sense of balance and a formidable self-assurance. Above all, a Wiccan's most distinguishing features are that they are happy, fulfilled and at peace with themselves.

When you are new to Wicca, you will probably find it difficult to juggle everything at once. There is the round of sabbats to celebrate (one every six weeks or so), another of esbats (one every full moon) and the seemingly endless list of things to make, do and learn. After that you still have to fit in work, romance, family, children and your own personal interests. One of the great strengths of Wicca, however, is that it encourages you to keep your feet firmly on the ground. Experience the divine by all means, be transported, but make sure that afterwards you can still pay the bills.

OUT OF THE BROOM CLOSET

On top of everything else, the question that besets most people who are new to Wicca is 'Should I tell anyone?' Ultimately, of course, everyone has to make his or her own decision, but it is wise to think very, very carefully indeed before announcing to the world in general that you are a witch. It is only within the last fifty years, a mere blink of the eye, that witchcraft has been decriminalized. It is even more recently, within the last twenty years or so, that witchcraft has begun to lose some of its traditional stigma.

If you are determined to declare your beliefs, it is probably easiest to start with your friends. After all, they love you for who you are and they may already share some of your interests or, at least, have an inkling of what interests you.

If you do tell them you are a witch, you must be prepared for the possibility that they might not like it. People generally don't like change and may not accept your behaving in a new way. Point out to any of your friends who seem angry or derisive about your news that you are still the same person. Just because you have chosen a particular spiritual path does not mean you have given up your ability to make rational decisions. You may want to mention that Wicca is all about considering your actions rather than blindly following a faith or a guru.

Right
Meditation, both at home and in the countryside, forms a large part of every witch's journey of self-discovery.

Below
Priest and priestess perform a simple candle spell in the woods.

FAMILY

Telling your family of your choice is fraught with a whole new set of problems. If you come from a strongly Christian background, you may find it is more trouble than it is worth to announce suddenly that you are a witch. If you simply must tell them, pave the way by breaking your family in gently to the new you. Let them know of your growing interest in nature, say, or folk traditions. Introduce the subject as Wicca, which is more neutral, rather than witchcraft. You may find it sensible to leave things pretty vague. Your devout, church-going grandparents, for example, will not want to imagine you naked, invoking the Horned God, or frolicking around a bonfire in the moonlight.

WORK

Telling colleagues at work is probably the trickiest decision of all, and you may in any case feel it is not the business of anyone at your workplace to know about your private spiritual beliefs. Think more than twice about telling your colleagues if you are in a field that is traditionally very conservative, such as banking or insurance. If you are a doctor, lawyer or teacher, you may well feel that you should keep your religious beliefs to yourself. Never forget it is an honourable tradition in magic to 'keep silent'.

CHILDREN

If you have children, it is likely they will already know of your interest in Wicca, even if you haven't told them. Children pick up on these things, so it's always better to be open with them. If your children are still very young, it is probably best to explain that Wicca is about connecting with nature and celebrating the seasons.

Your children will either shrug and treat Wicca as yet another of your weird parental habits, in which they have no interest, or they will want to know more. You can certainly share a celebration of the year and a sense of the Goddess and God, but do be careful. Most Wiccans would say that anyone under the age of 18 is probably still too young to become fully involved in Wicca as a spiritual path. In order to follow Wicca, you need to have some life experience behind you.

Every Wiccan parent has to decide whether to inform their child's school or not. Depending on the kind of school your child attends, you may find it wiser to remain vague about your spirituality. If, for some reason, the information does come out, don't deny it. Within the law you have as much right to practise your religion as anyone else. The best defence against bigotry and ignorance is to know your rights and to explain them to the school, clearly and with conviction.

Left
Wiccans often leave offerings in sacred places. These chimes hang above a Bronze Age labyrinth.

Right
A solar God symbol used in a crop-blessing ceremony.

The Urban Witch

Many people who are new to Wicca still have the mistaken belief that, in order to really live like a witch, they have to have a cottage in the wilds, a garden full of herbs for potion-making and a hand-reared weasel as a familiar. That's not how it works. Wiccans live in the real world and that means having a job and paying bills just like everyone else.

The vast majority of Wiccans are city witches who live in apartments in large urban developments. A surprising number of witches are involved in the world of computers, the Internet and IT, while many more are nurses, psychotherapists and analysts.

These witches work in centrally heated offices, far removed from the elements, they can barely see the night sky because of light pollution and they walk on pavements several feet thick. So how do city witches manage to stay in touch with the changing rhythms of the earth? The answer is that they can, because they learn to be creative in the way they approach their environments.

First, city witches use their senses. They look for signs of magic wherever they are and they know how to interpret them. The casual observer will simply see the small nettle, sprouting up through the ground by the bus stop, as a weed and nothing more. The witch will know it magically. They will recognize the nettle as a herb of the God – its sharp sting a reminder of the lighting bolt that strikes into the womb of the earth with the power to fertilize the land.

MAGIC IN THE STREET

The poet John Betjeman once said that to discover the best architecture one should always look up. This is something urban witches often do, for above the plastic advertising hoardings and shop fronts of the high street there are still signs of the old gods. Older British buildings are often adorned with carved images of the Green Man, with nymphs, dryads, the fruit and flowers of the Goddess or the pipes of Pan – reminders of the powers of nature that surround us.

City witches also use their intuition and seek out information about the magical history of the area in which they live. They may be drawn to particular sites that are below feet of concrete, but, for them, still resonate with power. Searching through old maps may reveal them as the sites of holy wells, streams, groves or beacon hills. Place names often give clues. Billingsgate, for example, the most prosaic of London's markets, was once Belen's Gate, the gate that honoured the sun God and the path of his rising over the city.

Another simple way that urban witches connect with the rhythms of nature is to plant window boxes and to make regular visits to parks and gardens. Spending time tending herbs or watching something as ordinary as a park squirrel still connects us to the natural world. The closer you look, the more you see and the deeper your connection with the earth becomes.

Finally, many city-dwelling witches become involved in schemes that aim to rejuvenate or to conserve the wildlife and green spaces of urban centres. Through volunteering to help conserve natural areas, witches are both contributing to their communities and fulfilling their own need to connect with the earth.

Right
Even a public park can provide an opportunity for the urban witch to encounter nature.

Solo Practice

There are two choices that every would-be witch must make – whether to try to find a coven or training group to join, or to work alone. If you are completely new to the craft you may feel that you want to get your bearings before rushing to try to join a group. This is a sound plan. Making a commitment to Wicca is a huge step and one best undertaken only after you have a solid understanding of what is involved. Many people choose to work alone while they are learning about the craft.

FREEDOM

There are lots of benefits to working alone. First and probably most important is the freedom to do whatever you like. With no one else there you can dance as wildly as you want, sing – in or out of tune – try any kind of ritual you fancy and generally let yourself go. You could find that, as there is nothing between you and your Gods, the experience of working alone is very intense and immediate.

The opposite side of the coin is that there is no one to help you and advise you and no one with whom to share your discoveries. Some find working as a solitary can be quite lonely. There is also the question of how much power you generate. Working alone means you generate your own amount of power and that is it. Working in a coven is synergistic. It produces a quantity of power that is much greater than the sum of its parts. Neither way is better than the other – they simply produce different amounts of energy.

You may feel that a coven might be restrictive in various ways. In one sense, it is – there's no getting away from the fact that, as a new initiate, you pretty much have to do as you're told. You can't make autonomous decisions about how you worship or celebrate with the group and you have to take other people's ideas and preferences into account.

On the other hand, when you are part of a coven you have the opportunity to experience the intense bonds of love and friendship that grow up between members. Wiccans often talk about the 'group mind'

Above
Working alone means you can connect with the elements, the Goddess and the God in an intensely personal way.

of a coven and this is something that you really can't experience anywhere else. Through working magic and creating rituals together, the consciousness of each member of the coven becomes linked, so that, when in a circle, all are working together in harmony to achieve the same ends.

GETTING THE TIMING RIGHT

There may be some very practical reasons why you want to try working alone. Joining a coven takes an enormous amount of time and energy and not everyone is at a stage of their lives when they are able to make such a commitment. There are issues such as work, study and relationships. If, for example, you have just embarked on new career or a university degree, or have just fallen madly in love, your mind is unlikely to be fully focused on Wicca.

There are also valid emotional and developmental reasons for working alone. Wicca is a path of spiritual growth. Its followers need to be self-aware, balanced and responsible for their actions. If you are new to Wicca you will need to take time to come to terms with your emotional 'baggage' and to get to know yourself as a magical being.

Everyone goes through the same process, or at least they should do, if they hope to achieve any kind of personal development. A coven should not be a therapy group, nor is it the right forum for the public exploration of an individual's personal problems. While coven leaders and other members are sympathetic and caring, a coven should be devoted, primarily, to making magic and the worship of the Gods. In the end each of us is ultimately accountable for our own mental and spiritual health, we are our own responsibility.

Wicca exposes our shortcomings rather than disguising them. If we are honest we will recognise and face them. We will work to correct our problems and then move on. The Wiccan path is not an easy one, particularly for the solo practitioner, but it is an empowering one. If you pursue it to the utmost of your ability you will find yourself and your life transformed.

Experiencing Ritual

THE MAGIC CIRCLE

All Wiccan rituals take place within a magic circle, which exists as a space set apart from the everyday world. Wiccans venerate the earth and consider it sacred. When they cast a circle, they are not trying to sanctify or in some way improve the physical ground on which they work. Instead they aim to create a separate space that exists between the world of men and the realms of the Gods. When Wiccans talk about 'cleansing' a circle they are talking about excluding any unnecessary or counterproductive influences.

Whatever their form and content, all Wiccan rituals exist within 'the circle, squared', that is to say in a magic circle, within which is a square created by the open portals of the four compass points of east, south, west and north. In undertaking a ritual, the priest or priestess casts a circle that encloses and contains the magical energy produced there. The magic circle also echoes the great cosmic circle of the universe. Having 'opened the quarters', the witch is able to work at the meeting point of earth, air, fire and water. Each time such rituals are undertaken, they re-establish within each priest and priestess a sense of balance and harmony with the cosmos.

THE UNCONSCIOUS MIND

The point of any ritual, whether it is a complicated one involving tools, altars and robes, or a simple circle in the woods, is that it alters your state of consciousness. Because ritual works with symbols, and the unconscious mind recognizes symbols rather than language, the way in which a ritual is constructed means it affects the unconscious mind immediately and deeply.

Rituals often involve repetition, rhythm and sets of symbolic actions or movements. This could be something as simple as ritual sweeping, or the more complicated acts of casting the circle or opening the quarters. Ritual allows the witch to bypass everyday habits and inhibitions and quickly reach a state of heightened consciousness.

Whatever the ritual contains, whether dancing, incense, visualization or chanting, these movements, scents, sights and sounds will act as triggers to prepare the mind for the magical work that is to follow. Often, the most effective rituals are the simplest ones, in which every action, symbol or magical tool helps to reinforce the intent of those taking part.

Wiccan rituals offer a way to combine regular religious observance (marking the seasons and honouring the Divine) with acknowledgement of an individual's own periods of growth, transition and achievement. As well as the normal round of esbats and sabbats, there are rituals to welcome new babies (known by some as 'Wiccaning'), rituals to unite couples in marriage (hand-fasting) and rituals that honour and celebrate the lives of those who go through the gates of death before us.

Honouring the Goddess

MAIDEN, MOTHER, CRONE

Wiccans honour the divine feminine in the form of the Triune or Triple Goddess whose three aspects of Virgin, Mother and Wise Woman correspond to the phases of the moon. As each successive moon waxes, grows full and wanes to darkness, Wiccans re-establish their relationship both with the Goddess and with the archetypal phases of female existence.

FACES OF THE GODDESS

While modern Wiccans willingly revere an eclectic range of Goddesses, from Roman Diana to Egyptian Isis or Greek Hecate, they venerate these Goddesses as the Maiden, Mother and Crone aspects of the One Divine Female. While all goddesses can be approached in their own right and have their own gifts and insights to offer, each one is ultimately a face of the Great Goddess. The essence of the Goddess is the contradictory premise that, while she constantly appears in different guises, she is always the same. That is what makes the moon so appropriate as her symbol. Like her, the moon shows us various aspects throughout each month and yet remains unchanged.

As life after life, season after season and moon after moon circle endlessly round, we come to understand that the energy of the Goddess is fundamentally cyclical. Wiccans hold their rituals and work their magic by the light of the moon, in the hope of gaining deeper access to these circular tides of energy. They also hope to develop their unconscious minds and to heighten their intuitive faculties, all of which are considered by some Wiccans as 'gifts of the Goddess'.

This eternal cycle shows us the crucial difference between the Goddess and the God. In many traditions a new God comes forward every winter solstice, in order to make an autumnal sacrifice of his blood to fertilize the harvest. As Stewart Farrar points out in *The Goddess of the Witches*, while it is accepted that the Goddess's fecundity is renewed by the fertilizing power of each successive God, there is never the suggestion that the Goddess herself could die. Certainly she sleeps through the winter and when she does so the productivity of the land ceases; but she always wakes renewed in spring, her life-giving power undiminished.

Wiccans approach the cyclical energies of the Goddess in different ways. Some simply see the changing seasons of the year as stages in the 'life' of the Goddess. In spring they honour her as the virgin, returning to earth restored; in summer she is the mother, mature, sensual and sexually productive; and in autumn and winter she takes on the qualities of the wise woman. Others view the seasonal differences as symbolic of the more complex tides of the earth's energy.

WORKING WITH THE GODDESS

The fact that the Goddess has so many faces enables witches to explore varying facets of their own personalities. For example, all men and women have within them, like the virgin, the ability to renew themselves, to move forward emotionally and to see the world afresh. Similarly all of us have the capacity to conceive, give birth and nurture to maturity.

This may be the act of becoming pregnant, giving birth and raising a child; or it may be seeing through a new venture from seed idea to completion. Whatever our sex or age, the creative force of the mother is open to all of us. In the same way, everyone, both male and female, can explore the mysteries of the crone. It is one of the truly great accomplishments of life to come to terms with the energy of the wise woman, to learn to respect and to stop fearing death.

Right
In the womb-like darkness of a crystal cave, a priestess explores the subtle energies of the Mother Goddess.

Below
If you work magic at ancient sites, make sure you leave no trace, such as candle wax or soot. Any offerings you leave should be biodegradable.

Women and Wicca

Right
Even the smallest space can be used as an altar. This one is dedicated to Aphrodite.

Below
Whenever possible, witches celebrate outdoors. These priestesses are returning from a Beltane rite.

Wicca is almost unique among Western spiritual traditions in that it offers women a role of power, strength and dignity. Even today, in many religions women are seen as servants or as unavoidable encumbrances. Christianity, for example, early put forward the idea that women embodied the physical and the sensual, considered to be the 'non-spiritual' aspects of humankind; and for centuries Christian Church fathers deemed women to be inherently sinful and corrupting. Conversely, men were promoted as creatures of spirit, able to push aside the body's needs to devote themselves purely to ethereal pursuits.

This dislocation of body and spirit has proven unsatisfying for many women, of Christian and other faiths, who have turned to Wicca to find a connection between the earthy, the sensual and

the spiritual. In Wicca, priestesses are not servants; they play an equal role in consecrating the circle and those present at the ritual, and it is always the priestess who actually casts the circle, creating the magical space between the worlds.

It is accepted that, within the craft, women can and do hold positions of considerable power. No one sees it as a conflict of interest for a woman to have a job and a family and to take on the responsibility of running a coven. In fact all women are encouraged to experience as much as they can of life, both within and outside the craft. Within the craft, the older a woman becomes the more she is respected and valued.

THE POWER WITHIN

Choosing Wicca gives women the opportunity to gain access to their own strength – as Stewart Farrar puts it, to 'waken the sleeping power within' – and to fulfil their potential, not just spiritually but practically and emotionally as well.

Many women find that Wicca gives them greater scope to explore their femininity. This can often be an illuminating process. Some Wiccans, who have only seen themselves as wives, mothers or dutiful daughters, are amazed to discover that they may have a warrior spirit within.

The opposite can also be true. There are those who may have battled through life alone and who consider themselves ready for 'cronedom'. These women may be shocked to learn that not only do they carry within themselves the maiden's innocence or the mother's sensuality, but that they have access to this knowledge and can learn to use it magically. Along with a growing sense of what it means to be female comes a discovery of the inner masculine, or as Jung describes it, the animus, that lies within each woman. Wicca provides a structure that helps to balance and reconcile these opposites.

Wicca offers every woman the chance to break free of the constraints of the everyday world. She is offered a route to ecstasy, to experience 'outside' the body, via invocation, trance and visualization. In this ecstatic state all women are able to commune directly with the Gods.

THE ROLE OF THE PRIESTESS

Finally, and perhaps most importantly, Wicca gives women a powerful role in the world. When you become a priestess of Wicca – whether you are initiated or simply dedicate yourself to the Craft of the Wise – you become a representative of the Goddess on earth. If you take this role seriously then you must begin to behave accordingly, in a way that is true to your higher self and accords respect to the Goddess. As a priestess there should be no room for fear, for self-indulgence, or for carelessness in your life.

In her book, *The Complete Art of Witchcraft*, Sybil Leek gives some useful pointers for would-be priestesses. 'A witch,' she writes, 'must not fall into any misfortune she can avoid. Nor must she fail at what she sets her will to achieve.' She goes on to suggest that a witch's life should be 'balanced and orderly', that she should 'seek safety from delusion and apprehension' and that she should exhibit 'tolerance, self-confidence and conviction', in both her public and private life.

This is a very tall order, but certainly something to which we should all aspire. While we are only human and as prone to making mistakes as anyone else, as witches we should be trying, in every aspect of our lives, to honour our Gods.

Aspects of the Goddess

CELTIC GODDESSES

Arianrhod
The Welsh Goddess of fertility and reincarnation. She is often described in Wicca as the 'Silver Wheel', or the 'Keeper of the Spiral Castle'. She dwells in Caer Arianrhod, which lies beyond the Aurora Borealis.

Blodeuwedd
A Welsh floral Goddess, Blodeuwedd was created out of flowers as a partner for the fertility God Lugh. She is often known as 'Flower Face' or 'White Flower'.

Cailleach Bheur
A Scottish Goddess, the Cailleach is one of the destroyer aspects of the Great Goddess. She is also known as Scota and Scotland is named after her. The Cailleach rules during winter and ensures that nothing grows between the sabbats of Samhain and Beltane.

Cerridwen
Known in both Scotland and Wales, Cerridwen is a Goddess of the Moon, of nature and of transformation.

Modron
Another Welsh Goddess, Modron means 'divine mother'. Of all mother Goddesses in Celtic history, Modron is perhaps the most powerful.

The Morrigan
Known throughout the Celtic world, The Morrigan or Morrigu reigns over the battlefield. She does not incite war, but appears over the field of battle in the form of a raven.

Such is the great power of The Morrigan that she is known by a number of different names, including 'Supreme War Goddess', 'Spectre Queen', 'Great Mother' and 'Great White Goddess'. She is also considered by some to be the patron deity of witches.

GREEK GODDESSES

Aphrodite
Goddess of Love. Her name means 'She of the heavens' and Aphrodite represents the driving life force of the universe.

Artemis
Goddess of the Moon and symbol of the untamed in nature, Artemis is often depicted as a virgin huntress. Her arrows supposedly have the power both to protect and destroy. The temple of Artemis at Ephesus was one of the wonders of the ancient world.

Athena
Goddess of Wisdom and of War, protector of the city of Athens. Athena is the patron Goddess of spinning, weaving and pottery as well as being a protector of children, women and warriors.

Demeter
Goddess of the Harvest and mother of Persephone. When Persephone was taken to the Underworld, Demeter withdrew her abundance from the earth and all plants withered. Demeter represents fertility and the changing of the seasons.

Hera
Great Mother Goddess.

Persephone
Daughter of Demeter. Abducted by Hades and taken to the Underworld as his wife, Persephone was eventually freed, but has to remain with Hades for three months of the year. While her daughter is in the Underworld, Demeter grieves and the earth is barren.

Roman Goddesses

Diana
The Roman version of Artemis, Diana is the Virgin Goddess of the moon, of hunting and the protector of wild animals.

Juno, Queen of Heaven
The Roman version of the Mother Goddess Hera, Juno is the patron Goddess of marriage, motherhood and childbirth. She is also considered to be a giver of wise counsel.

Minerva
Roman version of the Athena. A Goddess of wisdom, war and the protector of the city of Rome, Minerva is also the patron Goddess of crafts, drama and the arts.

Babylonian/Sumerian Goddesses

Inanna – also known as Ishtar
Inanna/Ishtar is the Great Goddess. She also represents fertility, love, war and descent into the Underworld.

Nintu
Mother of all Gods and partner of Father God Anu, Nintu is credited with creating mankind from the earth.

Tiamat
Tiamat represents primeval chaos and creation. Tiamat was destroyed by her children in a battle and the resulting chaos created the world.

Egyptian Goddesses

Hathor
Hathor is the daughter of Nuit and is known as 'The house (or womb) of Horus' – one of her roles is to protect Horus. Hathor also has a destructive role and, when in it, appears as a snake. She is a patron Goddess of fertility, childbirth and of the dead. In this aspect she is known as the 'Lady of the West'.

Isis
Mother Goddess – wife of Osiris and mother of Horus, Isis represents the sovereignty or 'throne' of the pharaohs. Isis is also a Goddess of the dead and was responsible for reassembling the body of Osiris after his death. She is known as 'The Star of the Sea'.

Maat
Goddess of truth and universal harmony. Maat is often depicted wearing an ostrich feather (or simply as the feather itself) and judging the souls of the dead before they passed into the Underworld.

Nuit
Goddess of the Heavens, Nuit is often shown as a woman whose body reaches up and over the world, creating the arch of the sky. Ra, the Sun God, entered Nuit's mouth each evening to be reborn every morning.

Below
A priestess invokes Blodeuwedd, a Celtic flower goddess.

Honouring the God

Like the Goddess, the God has several aspects and these highlight his primary functions as a deity of hunting, protection and the underworld and as a solar/vegetation spirit.

THE HORNED ONE

The Horned God of the hunt is the older of the two roles, hunting having preceded agriculture by thousands of years. One of the earliest and most well-known images of the Horned One can be found at the Cavern des Trois Frères, at Ariège in France. This cave painting shows a human figure draped in animal skins and wearing a set of large antlers. It seems highly likely that the figure depicts either a hunter taking on the magical persona of the prey or a shaman opening himself to the vital energy of the God of the Hunt.

This hunting divinity ruled the natural forces of life and death and in time became associated with both hunting and culling and came to symbolize the hunter and the prey.

Wiccans worship the Horned God as Cernunnos. In ancient bone and metal carvings, the most famous of which is the Gundestrup cauldron, Cernunnos is shown bearing the stag's antlers and often wearing a torc of gold. He is also frequently shown surrounded by serpents and by bags of gold. His association with these chthonic symbols of the underworld signals his own connection with the dead. Over time Cernunnos has become not just a symbol of the sacrificial stag, but the 'Keeper of the Gateway of Death', whose task it is to guide us from this world to the next.

The Horned God also manifests himself as Pan or Faunus. In this form he appears as a horned man above the waist and as a cloven-hoofed goat below. He is a primary symbol of the connection between man, the creative power of nature and the divine. In Wicca, the young God is seen as the 'phallic hunter' whose lustful chase and capture of the Goddess ensures her fertility.

THE CORN KING

As agriculture overtook hunting as the main method of food production, the more recent God aspect emerged – that of the solar/vegetation spirit, who ensures the productivity of agricultural land. He is the son and consort of the Goddess; he gains in strength as the sun's power increases and fades and dies as the sun's power wanes.

In mythology this God figure is often shown conquering his father. In Irish mythology, for example, the myth of Lugh symbolizes the protection of the fertility of farmland. Lugh vanquishes his grandfather Balor who represents the wild and untamed force of nature. Balor's symbolic aim is to lay waste agricultural land and return it to its natural, forest state. In defeating him, Lugh drives back the wilderness and claims the fields and their harvest for mankind.

As a vegetation spirit, the God sacrifices himself for the fertility of the crops, allowing himself to be beheaded (in a symbolic acknowledgement of the regenerative power of plants which, when picked, grow stronger) and his blood to fall on the land. The potency of this sacrificial king is intimately linked with the potency of the sun. Thus, as the sun rises to its zenith at the midsummer solstice, so the power of the solar king rises. After the solstice, however, when the sun's power starts to wane, the solar king sacrifices himself in order to make room for a new sun/king to be born at the midwinter solstice.

In ancient cultures, kings often gained their authority through marriage to the indigenous queen of the area – an embodiment of the power of the Goddess. Without a formal sexual union with the queen, who was seen as the incarnation

Above
An offering to the sacrificial Corn King.

of the land, the king held no real power. It is possible that the king may also have performed a ceremonial act of mating with the earth itself.

It is thought that after a period of seven years, the king was ritually slaughtered and his blood offered to the land to ensure its productivity. This constant stream of new blood was believed to maintain the earth's fertility. Scholars suggest that when a queen became too old to procreate she passed the title down to her daughter, re-enforcing the ongoing and undying qualities of the land.

In Wicca the two personas of the vegetation spirit are revered as the Oak King and the Holly King. The Oak King rules while the sun is gaining in power. After the midsummer solstice the Holly King rules, when the sun is waning.

Above
Bearing the symbol of
Cernunnos, the Horned
One, a priestess welcomes
the dawn.

Wicca and Men

Wicca offers men the same benefits as are offered to women – a variety of strong archetypal role models, a route to ecstatic communion with the divine and a set of flexible traditions, which enable each individual to empower their lives.

Today, the role of men in Wicca seems to be increasingly overlooked by both the media and the general public. When Gerald Gardner first came into the craft he claimed that the percentage of men in Wicca was much higher than that of women. Many had turned to witchcraft from predominantly male areas such as freemasonry and ceremonial magic.

THE ROLE OF THE MEDIA

Over the years the number of women in Wicca has drawn level and now greatly supersedes the number of men. Recently this has been due, in no little part, to the role played by film and television. Films such as *Charmed* and *The Craft* and mainstream television series such as *Buffy the Vampire Slayer* and *Sabrina the Teenage Witch* portray Wiccans and witches in a superficial way and only ever as teenage girls. While some sources claim that Wicca is the fastest-growing spiritual path of this century, there seem to be no current media models of male witches.

If, however, you ask any of the men now practising Wicca in Britain why they are drawn to the craft, you will hear strong affirmations of the validity of this path for men. Wicca allows men access to a spirituality that, unlike many other religions, makes room for sensuality, wildness and strength alongside wisdom and spiritual aspiration. Wicca does not deny, or classify as 'sinful', the sexual and sensual attributes of the personality. In contrast it celebrates the dynamic, creative power engendered by these emotions. The Horned God is neither celibate nor cerebral. He is of the earth, potent and untamed. This is not to say that he is

incapable of wisdom – the Horned God is profoundly wise, but it is a wisdom of the earth and of the deep tides of nature.

Men who come to Wicca may find that they are able to explore their previously unknown feminine qualities and to discover more about their anima (or inner female). They are often taken aback at the depths of tenderness and empathy they discover, characteristics that inevitably make them more resilient and better balanced both as men and as witches.

Wiccan priests, who choose to dedicate their lives to the worship of the Goddess and the God, find themselves in the same position as the priestesses mentioned in the previous chapter. If they hope to represent the God on earth, priests must – and invariably do – bring about any necessary changes in their lives.

It is unacceptable for Wiccan priests to behave carelessly, or to be dominated by their fears. Like his female counterpart, the priest must accept responsibility for his actions and learn to rely on himself and his inner force – to share the strength and wisdom of the God through his own personal example.

Above
An altar dedicated to Cernunnos displays the antlers and oak leaves of the God, alongside quartz and fluorite crystals to heighten spiritual awareness.

Left
Wiccan priests follow a path that encourages both spirituality and sensuality, wisdom and strength.

Aspects of the God

GREEK GODS

Pan
Fertility deity who symbolizes the union of man and nature. From the waist up Pan is human, from the waist down he is goat. He is the patron God of shepherds and their flocks.

Dionysus
Although ostensibly the God of wine and fertility, Dionysus is one of the most important Greek deities and became associated with the themes of death and rebirth. His worship was originally orgiastic and Dionysus was invariably attended by a company of revelling nymphs and satyrs.

His symbol is the pine cone thyrsus or wand, wound round with a double strand of ivy. Over time the ivy evolved into the twin snakes of Hermes' caduceus.

Zeus
Great Father God.

NORSE GODS

Odin
Odin is the most important God in the Norse pantheon, patron of wisdom, poetry, magic and war. Odin sacrificed himself on Ygdrassil (the World Tree) for nine days and nights in order to gain wisdom. He also sacrificed an eye to Mimir, payment so that he could drink at Mimir's spring and remember everything in the world.

CELTIC GODS

Cernunnos
Lord of the Animals and Guardian of the Gates of Death, Cernunnos is Lord of the Underworld. His antlers signify his divinity and affinity with nature. Cernunnos is often shown with ram-headed serpents and bags of money, confirming his links to the Underworld.

Lugh
God of thunderstorms and lightning, Lugh symbolizes the fertilizing power of the sun. His weapon is the magic spear.

Dagda
The Dagda was the Great Father God of the tribe of Dana in Ireland. He is famed for his magic cauldron, which never empties. The Dagda is also responsible for ensuring that the seasons turn to the music of his harp.

EGYPTIAN GODS

Anubis
The son of Nephthys and Osiris, Anubis is often depicted with the head of a jackal. Anubis, in his role as 'pathfinder', leads the dead on their journey to the underworld.

Osiris
Husband of the Goddess Isis, Osiris is the judge of the dead in the underworld. Osiris was killed by his brother Set, who cut his body into many pieces. Isis reassembled her husband's body and then impregnated herself with his semen to become the mother of Horus.

Horus
An Egyptian sky god, Horus is usually shown as a falcon and the sun and moon were thought to be his eyes. Egyptian pharaohs claimed their authority from Isis and Horus and believed that each pharaoh becomes Horus on their deaths. Horus lost an eye during a battle and presented it to his father Osiris. The image of a human eye surrounded by the feathered markings of the falcon, known as the 'Eye of Horus' is still used today as a protective amulet.

Ra

The Egyptian Sun God, Ra is shown as a man with a falcon's head, crowned with the sun disc and a sacred cobra. In Egyptian mythology, Ra travels the ocean of the sky in a solar boat. Those who looked up and saw the sun's progress believed they were seeing the god moving across the sky. Each night he passes into the Goddess Nuit's mouth and through her body, which represents the Underworld, to be reborn each morning.

Thoth

The Egyptian God of learning, Thoth is shown with the head of an ibis. He was also worshipped as a baboon. It was Thoth who originally gave humankind the art of writing and was the patron God of languages, law and mathematics.

SUMERIAN/BABYLONIAN GODS

Dumuzi

Dumuzi features in the Bible as Tammuz. He is a shepherd who mates with the Goddess Inanna to ensure the fertility of the land.

In a variation on the Persephone myth, Inanna allows Dumuzi to be taken into the underworld for half of the year (which corresponds to the barren, desert-like months of the Sumerian summer) so that she can remain on earth. Dummuzi returns to earth at each autumn equinox, Inanna rejoices, and animals and plants began to reproduce once more.

Marduk

Marduk is primarily a fertility God. In myth, he vanquished the creation Goddess Tiamat, whose death created the earth. His power grew until he was recognized as a Great Father God and a creator of life and light.

Marduk eventually became known simply as Bel or Lord.

Above
A priest invokes the fertility God Lugh as the year turns and the sun's power fades.

The Element of Air

THE ELEMENTS

In Wicca, every magic circle contains the energy of the four classical elements of air, fire, water and earth. Each of these powers is drawn (or invoked) into the circle in turn, in order to establish a magical working space that is open to the primary forces of the cosmos. Each of the elements is ascribed a direction or point on the compass and so, as each elemental portal is opened, the witch stands at the meeting point of these cardinal energies, in harmony with the universe.

Each of the elements has a set of magical and physical correspondences. These magical parallels resonate with and allow us access to the energy of a given element.

Of all the elements, air is perhaps the best symbol for magic. We can't see air, or feel it or touch it, and yet we know it is there because we breathe it in every minute – it sustains us and keeps us alive.

Magically, air rules the functions of the mind. This includes all mental activity, including abstract thought, theorizing, communication and knowledge. It brings with it inspiration, purification, change and the ability to make new beginnings. On a physical level air rules breathing, speech, sound and harmony.

Many Wiccans ascribe human characteristics to the energies of each of the quarters. For most people, this makes them easier to approach and to contact. These elemental guardians are often known as the 'Gatekeepers' or 'Guardians of the Watchtowers'. The gatekeeper of air can be seen as a blond youth, or even a child, standing in the east. He is traditionally dressed in a cape of pale yellow or blue feathers and carries either a bow and quiver of arrows or a sword.

ENCOUNTERING THE ELEMENT OF AIR

In order to gain access to the magical realms, it is necessary to be able to see them with your inner eye – to visualize them. Magical visualization is examined later in this book, but for now you simply need to be able to relax and allow yourself to build up a picture in your mind's eye.

Find a comfortable position, still your mind and slow your breathing. Picture the dawn and see yourself looking toward the rising sun in the east. Imagine a large five-pointed star of pale blue flame floating before you. Trace an air-invoking pentagram with your finger (see diagram, left). To one side of the pentagram, the gatekeeper of air appears. See him standing before you. He is a young man with pale blond hair. He is dressed in a cloak of yellow and blue feathers, which flutter in the faint breeze that surrounds him. He is carrying a short sword. Wait for the gatekeeper of air to pull back the veil between our world and the other realms. Follow him as he steps through the portal into the domain of air.

Spend some time in this new world. You may encounter winged elemental beings such as sylphs. They may grant you gifts or answer your questions.

When it is time to return, thank any guides or elemental beings you have encountered. Step back through the portal into our world. Thank the gatekeeper of air and cast an air-closing pentagram (see diagram, top left), sometimes called a banishing pentagram. After your elemental journey, eat and drink something to ground yourself and bring you fully back to your body.

INVOKING
PENTAGRAM

BANISHING
PENTAGRAM

Above right
Experiencing air directly and personally will radically improve your understanding of the inspirational qualities of the element.

Right
All pipes and flutes correspond to the element of air. The action of blowing a breath through a wind instrument brings it to life and gives it a voice.

MAGICAL CORRESPONDENCES FOR AIR

Direction	East	**Images**	Knives, swords, arrows, science, analysis, mountains, feathers, mirrors, wind instruments, perfume, poets, singers, teachers, books, scrolls, computers
Season	Spring		
Point in life	Childhood/youth		
Time of day	Sunrise		
Elemental beings	Sylphs		
Colour	Yellow/pale blue	**Contacting air**	Listen to wind chimes, bells, whistles and flutes. On a windy day, climb a hill and feel the air rushing past you. Chant aloud and analyze the different resonances of the sounds. Try breathing exercises, which make you aware of each breath. Try some IQ tests or mental puzzles.
Magical virtue	To know		
Magical tools	Athame, sword, censer		
Archangel	Raphael		
Jewel	Quartz, diamonds and topaz		
Astrological rulers	Mercury		
Wind of the East	Eurus		
Zodiac signs	Gemini, Libra and Aquarius		
Tarot suit	Swords		
Essential oils	Lavender, lemon, violet, rosemary, frankincense	**Goddesses of air**	Arianrhod, Athena, Minerva, Nuit
Creatures	All birds and winged insects	**Gods of air**	Enlil, Mercury, Hermes, Thoth
Plants	Lavender, marjoram, mint and caraway		
Trees	Hazel, aspen		

△ The Element of Fire

Fire might be seen as the most contradictory of the elements. In one sense it is completely domestic – we use it to heat our homes and to cook our food. Warmth makes a home feel protected and the hearth fire or a warm kitchen is still the centre of most family life. Yet fire will burn us, even kill us, if we give it the opportunity. More than any other, this element has the quality of will. Given the chance, fire will range wherever it likes and, if uncontrolled, can consume everything it touches.

Magically, fire rules the tides of energy, passion and aspiration. It is an element of change and has the power both to create and to destroy. Fire dictates our use of magical will, our ability to transform and to achieve. Traditionally it is also a symbol of divinity, and numerous Gods and mythical heroes are shown with lambent crowns, or haloes, around their heads.

Physically, fire rules our enthusiasms and our sexual dynamism, or potency – in other words, fire gives us our passion for living. The energy of the element is devouring and intense and, like physical fire, can be difficult to control. If allowed to range unchecked, fire energy can express itself in extremes of lust, obsession and anger. It can easily destroy everything within its reach. However, when understood and controlled, fire energy can be illuminating in the most profound way.

ENCOUNTERING THE ELEMENT OF FIRE

The gatekeeper of fire can be seen as a mature man in the prime of his life. He is often visualized as having long, red hair and a luxuriant red beard. His skin is golden brown. The gatekeeper is tall, broad and physically very powerful. He wears a cape of scarlet and has gold torcs at his neck and wrists that are set with flashing red stones. He carries a spear or club.

Find a comfortable position, relax, still your mind and slow your breathing. See yourself standing on the edge of a southern desert. The sun is at its highest point overhead. Imagine a pentagram of brilliant crimson flame suspended in the air before you. Trace a fire-invoking pentagram (see diagram) with your finger. See the gatekeeper of fire appear. He is dressed all in red and gold and rubies glint at his neck and wrists. Fire licks around his hair and down along his arms to the point of the spear that he carries.

Wait for the gatekeeper to draw back the veil between the worlds and then step through the pentagram portal into the realm of fire. Be aware that on your visit nothing can hurt you in this realm. The heat may be great but the destructive aspect of fire cannot harm you. Spend time in the kingdom of fire. Explore its landscape – you may encounter fire elementals such as salamanders, you may receive gifts or answers to your questions.

When it is time to leave, thank any of the guides or elemental beings you have met and step back through the portal. Thank the gatekeeper and bid him farewell, then cast a fire-closing, or banishing, pentagram (see diagram).

Eat and drink something after your journey to ground yourself fully after the experience.

INVOKING
PENTAGRAM

BANISHING
PENTAGRAM

Right

In front of a fire of oak and ash branches, a priestess attunes to her magical will to seek illumination.

Far right

Flames represent our physical passions which, if allowed to run out of control, may consume everything they touch.

MAGICAL CORRESPONDENCES FOR FIRE

Direction	South	**Plants**	Heliotrope, sunflowers, basil, chillies, nettles
Season	Summer		
Point in life	Prime of life	**Trees**	Oak, ash
Time of day	Midday	**Images**	Life blood, flames, bonfires, candles, hearth fires, lamps, solar glyphs, the phallus, divine kingship, deserts, volcanoes, staffs and staves, infernos, the heart, courage, illumination, power
Colour	Red, orange, crimson, gold, white, all colours of flame		
Magical virtue	To will		
Magical tools	Wand, candle		
Jewel	Fire opal, red jasper, ruby, bloodstone, garnet, lava, quartz crystals, carnelian, tiger's eye, agates		
Astrological rulers	Sun, Mars, Jupiter	**Contacting fire**	Light a bonfire or barbecue and tend the flames. Visit a sauna or solarium, or simply sunbathe. Try candle magic. Exercise vigorously. Eat fiery foods such as curry, onions, garlic and chillies.
Archangel	Michael		
Wind of the south	Notus		
Elemental spirits	Salamanders		
Metals	Gold, brass		
Zodiac signs	Aries, Leo and Sagittarius	**Goddesses of fire**	Brigid, Freya, Hestia, Vesta
Tarot suit	Batons or wands	**Gods of fire**	Ra, Vulcan, Apollo, Baldur, Bel, Horus
Essential oils	Pine, basil, calendula		
Creatures	Lions, dragons, lizards, snakes		

▽ The Element of Water

The element of water rules our emotions; its energy is synthezising and accepting. Water awakens our powers of creativity, tenderness, emotional receptivity and our ability to adapt and heal.

Magically, water is the archetypal symbol of the Great Mother, from whose womb we emerged and in whose waters we were cradled. Water energy helps us gain access to our psychic power and its force is healing and regenerative. Like that of all the elements, the power of water needs to be kept in balance. If allowed too free a range, water's emotional force can lead to delusion, infatuation, instability and violent mood swings. Kept in balance however, water brings us serenity, tranquillity and sensitivity.

While air and fire are considered by some to be 'masculine' elements, water and earth are considered 'feminine'. This means that their energies operate in subtly different ways. Air and fire energy can be seen to be linear, active and outward facing. Water and earth energy are often considered to be receptive, cyclical and inward turning.

ENCOUNTERING THE ELEMENT OF WATER

In some traditions the gatekeepers are all male, but if you accept water and earth energies as having different (some would say 'feminine') qualities, then the gatekeepers of these realms should reflect those differences.

The gatekeeper of water can be seen as a mature, middle-aged woman. Her hair is auburn, her eyes grey-green. On her brow is a moonstone, surrounded by pearls.

INVOKING
PENTAGRAM

BANISHING
PENTAGRAM

MAGICAL CORRESPONDENCES FOR WATER

Direction	West	**Images**	Pools, streams, rivers, oceans, waterfalls, mothers, nurses, carers, translucent crystals, movement, mist, receptiveness, dark mirrors, holy wells, the womb, menstruation, cleansing, rain, storm, hurricane, ice, flood
Season	Autumn		
Point in life	Middle age		
Time of day	Evening/twilight		
Colour	Sea green, blue, aquamarine		
Magical virtue	To dare		
Magical tools	Cauldron, chalice		
Jewel	Aquamarine, pearl		
Astrological rulers	Venus, Moon		
Archangel	Raphael	**Contacting water**	Swim or take meditation baths. Spend time at the beach listening to the song of the sea. Book a session in a flotation tank, dig a pond in the garden, hire a 'weepy' video or go to a comedy club and allow your emotions free range. Examine your feelings when you eat 'emotional' food such as chocolate.
Wind of the west	Zephyrus		
Elemental spirits	Undines		
Metals	Silver, copper and quicksilver (mercury)		
Zodiac signs	Cancer, Pisces and Scorpio		
Tarot suit	Cups		
Essential oils	Jasmine, rose, vanilla, tuber rose, lily		
Creatures	All sea creatures, especially whales, dolphins and sea snakes		
Plants	Apple, rose, elder, blackberry	**Goddesses of water**	Aphrodite, Tiamat, Isis
		Gods of water	Manannan, Poseidon, Neptune
Trees	Alder, willow		

She is dressed in a silk cloak, which shimmers with all the greens, blues and aquamarines of the ocean. Around the hem mother-of-pearl, coral and shells have been worked in the shape of otters, fish and seaweed. The gatekeeper has with her a cauldron or large chalice of water.

Find a comfortable position, relax, still your mind and allow your breathing to slow. See yourself on the shore of the western ocean. It is late evening and the sun is beginning to sink into the sea. Visualize a pentagram of liquid green flame. Trace a water-invoking pentagram (see diagram) with your finger and wait as the gatekeeper appears. She is dressed all in green and her cloak is covered with a pale, dew-like sheen. Long strings of pearls hang around her neck and she is carrying a large, shallow bowl from which sea water pours in silver strands.

Wait for the gatekeeper to draw back the veil between the worlds, then follow her into the kingdom of water. You may see creatures you have never encountered before – water elementals such as undines, softly waving among the seaweed, mermaids or the mysterious 'water-horse', or kelpie.

Explore this element for as long as you need, then bid your guides farewell, thanking them for any gifts or messages they have given you. Follow the gatekeeper though the portal. Thank her for her presence, then cast a water-closing, or banishing, pentagram (see diagram).

Make sure you eat and, more importantly, drink something to ground yourself in this world after your journey.

Above
A chalice represents the womb of creation and transformation.

Left
Running water symbolizes the witch's continuing search for balance and equilibrium.

⏢ The Element of Earth

The energy of the element of earth is a slow, rhythmic pulse. It is the steady, green heartbeat of the Great Mother. Earth's power is patient, fertile, enduring and stable. It is also wise, just, severe and absolutely implacable.

Magically, the element of earth is protective and grounding. Through earth, magical work finds its physical manifestation. The power of earth enables witches to plan their rituals practically and to carry them through with scrupulous care. It is upon the disc of the pentacle, the magical tool of earth, that the salt water rests which is used to delineate the magic circle. In this sense earth is the foundation and the solid, material basis of ritual.

ENCOUNTERING THE ELEMENT OF EARTH

The gatekeeper of earth is the crone. She is an ancient figure, shrouded in black and adorned with the riches of the earth. Her long white hair flows down over her cloak, which is studded with obsidian and jet in labyrinthine patterns. Her bony wrists are weighted down with serpent-like bands of gold, amber and quartz. Hag stones hang on strips of leather around her neck. The gatekeeper carries a flat disc of dark crystal, on which magical symbols are inscribed.

Find a comfortable position, relax, still your mind and allow your breathing to slow. With your inner eye, picture yourself at the mouth of a deep cavern. It is midnight and you can just see by the light of the stars. There, in front of you, hangs a huge pentacle of amber flame. Trace an earth-invoking pentagram (see diagram)

INVOKING
PENTAGRAM

BANISHING
PENTAGRAM

Right
Timeless, enduring and strong, the energy of a standing stone can be absorbed by touch.

Below
A rocky shelf provides support, privacy and shelter during a meditation.

with your finger and wait for the gate-keeper of earth to appear. See the crone step forward. She moves with difficulty and is supported by a wolf and a bear. Her cloak is as black as the midnight sky and she is as silent as the dust on the cavern floor.

Wait for the crone to pull back the veil between the worlds and then step through the portal behind her. In the domain of the element of earth you will find yourself in the realm of 'green energies'. You may see fairies, brownies or elemental beings such as gnomes. You may find yourself in contact with the energies of plants and crystals. Explore the kingdom of earth. When it is time to return, thank your guides for any gifts or wisdom they may have given you. Follow the crone back through the portal, thank her for her guidance and then cast an earth-closing, or banishing, pentagram (see diagram).

Make sure that you eat something to ground yourself after your journey.

MAGICAL CORRESPONDENCES FOR EARTH

Direction	North	**Creatures**	Stags, serpents, wolves, bears
Season	Winter	**Plants**	Poppy, fern, barley, corn
Point in life	Old age	**Trees**	Beech (Queen of the Woods), cypress
Time of day	Midnight		
Colour	Black, brown, green 'earth tones'	**Images**	Caves, woodland groves, standing stones, forests, orchards, tombs, burrows, feasting, long barrows, pyramids
Magical virtue	To keep silent		
Magical tools	Pentacle, shield		
Jewel	All stones, in particular obsidian, jet and dark crystals	**Contacting earth**	Visit caves and long barrows, take walks in the woods and forests, walk a maze or labyrinth, take up pottery, study geology and archaeology.
Astrological rulers	Saturn, Earth		
Archangel	Auriel		
Wind of the north	Boreus		
Elemental spirits	Gnomes		
Metals	Iron	**Goddesses of earth**	Gaia, Demeter, Ceres, Persephone, Flora, Cerridwen, Blodeuwedd
Zodiac signs	Taurus, Virgo and Capricorn		
Tarot suit	Coins or pentacles	**Gods of earth**	Pan, Herne, Cernunnos, Dumuzi
Essential oils	Patchouli, vetiver, sage, cypress		

Chapter 2
PRACTICAL
MAGIC

Aleister Crowley famously described magic as 'the art of causing change to occur in conformity with will'. While undoubtedly a man with some very serious flaws in his character Crowley was, above all, a master magician. He managed to devote all of his adult life to the serious study of magic. His definition of magic might seem very daunting to the novice witch. Many of those who are new to magic fear they may never be able to 'make something happen' using magic alone – but almost everyone has the latent ability to work magic. Dion Fortune later amended Crowley's quote to describe magic as 'the art of causing changes in consciousness to occur in conformity with will', which means that absolutely everyone can work magic.

What witches aim to do is train themselves, using ritual and meditation, to enhance their natural magical abilities. Nearly everyone already has some psychic or clairvoyant ability, from something as simple as 'knowing' just before someone close to you phones, or having an affinity for games of chance, or the ability to pick up sensations about a place simply by walking into a room.

Through practice and ritual, witches learn to alter their state of consciousness, and that is where real magic lies. Everyone has this ability. When in a relaxed state the brain moves from its normal beta rhythm into various slower rhythms (alpha, theta and delta). These slower rhythms are associated with the right hemisphere of the brain and with the unconscious mind. They are found in people who are dreaming and are re-created in those who

are meditating or performing ritual. Thus, everyone who masters meditation and brings that altered state of consciousness to the rituals they undertake will be able to work magic. As we change from within, so we are able to affect our outer reality.

Witches use a wide variety of means to achieve their ends. Most have a collection of tools which they use to concentrate and direct magical energy. These usually include knives, swords, wands, cauldrons and shields (or pentacles), and they each correspond to the magical elements.

Many witches are familiar with the magical properties of plants and trees and are well versed in herbal healing. Nearly all have a natural aptitude for divination and use systems such as the tarot or runes for prediction. Most famously, witches use spells to work magic: from complicated incantations involving talismans and magical symbols to something very simple such as lighting a candle or tying a knot.

Most importantly, witches perform rituals during which they contact their Gods and work their magic. Rituals are planned so that each element resonates symbolically in the witch's subconscious. The more adept a witch becomes at entering these altered states of being, the more able he or she is to access the world of magic.

WHITE VERSUS BLACK MAGIC
In Wicca, magic is not considered black or white, good or bad. Magic is seen simply as a force. In the same way that electricity can be used to protect or to take life, so magic can work for both good and ill. The moral code of each witch should ensure that magic is put to good use.

Left
The essence of magic lies in an altered state of consciousness. This can be triggered by an atmospheric spot or by ritual action like lighting incense.

Below
Keeping a record of the most effective symbols, spells and incantations helps you to enter a 'magical' state more easily.

The Witch's Tools

THE TWO MOST IMPORTANT TOOLS

In many explanations of witches' tools and ritual kits, the two most important tools of all are often ignored – these are your own body and your personal ability to make magic.

If you treat your ritual knife or cauldron with love and care, surely you should devote as much attention to your physical body? This means learning to love your body and to treat it with respect. If you can't love yourself, you won't be able to accept yourself and if you can't accept yourself, you will impede your ability to make magic.

Magic takes absolute concentration. When casting a circle or invoking the Gods, a witch needs to focus completely on that task. It is essential to quieten the inner voice of self-consciousness. This is the voice that, during rituals, reminds us we should really exercise more; the voice that fears we may look foolish brandishing a magic wand or worries that, skyclad, we may look overweight or underweight. Self-consciousness stops concentration, so learning to accept our bodies as they are is the first step in stilling that niggling voice.

Witches should also devote time to listening to their bodies' needs. They should think about what they eat, how much exercise they take, how much sleep they need (not how much they get, but how much they need). They ought to assess how stress at work, or at home, is going to affect the magic they do.

If you want to work magic more effectively, consider what you could do to improve your well-being. This could be something as simple as finding time to meditate more regularly, or just changing your diet or exercise patterns. It doesn't matter how many tools you have, how expensive or how beautifully crafted they are – if you do not treat yourself with respect you will not reach your full magical potential.

VISUALIZATION

The next most important tool is the witch's ability to visualize. This is a skill that can be learned and it is essential that you do learn it, because visualization (or seeing with the inner eye) is one of the main ways that witches create magic.

In a circle, witches project images and symbols into the 'other realms' or 'the magical planes'. If this is done successfully, these images, be they of actions, Gods, elemental beings or intentions, take on their own magical reality. Visualization is the key to successful magic.

Obviously not everyone finds visualization easy. Some people process information more effectively aurally (through hearing) and others through feelings or through their intellect. These people may find that instead of seeing a movie-like projection of their intent, they may hear it, or simply feel the desired outcome taking place. These are acceptable alternatives and, if you find that no matter how hard you try, you can't visualize easily, it may be that you will hear, or feel, your intent instead and can project these sensations into the magical planes.

Traditionally, however, most witches use visualization and most people are able to learn to visualize quite well with a little practice. Once again, concentration is the key. Those who learn to focus totally on the symbol or image in hand are usually most able to see it in their mind's eye and to project it magically.

Right
Each of the witch's tools has both a ritual and a symbolic purpose in creating sacred space and contacting the Gods.

Below
Providing a solid foundation for magical work, the pentacle acts to 'ground' witches and help them concentrate.

Basic Working Tools

Above

The double-edged blade of the athame directs the energy used in casting a circle and consecrating the cakes and wine.

Below

This wand combines male and female attributes. It is twisted with honeysuckle, corresponding to the God and the Sun, and tipped with copper, which corresponds to the Goddess and to Venus.

THE ATHAME

Every traditional Wiccan should have a ritual knife, or athame, which is used not for cutting but for directing magical energy. In the UK people usually pronounce it Athaymee with the emphasis on the middle syllable; in America, it tends to be A-thahmay. Certain witchcraft traditions do not use knives, but Gardnerian and Alexandrian witches prefer to work with athames. An athame should be straight, with a double-edged blade and, most importantly, a black handle. The athame doesn't have to be very grand – just an ordinary kitchen knife will do, provided it 'feels' right in your hand. The athame is traditionally associated with air and is seen as a masculine tool.

In an ideal world we would all be able to fashion our own blades under the light of a full moon, but most of us have to buy them. I would suggest buying a new athame – if you buy a second-hand knife you have no idea what it may have been used for, before it came to you.

Whether your blade is new or second-hand, it is a good idea to cleanse it thoroughly before use. Clean the blade with a metal polish and the hilt with a damp cloth, then dry the athame completely. Plunge it into a large bowl filled with salt or, alternatively, push the blade into the earth. Leave it in place for at least 12 hours. After that you can consecrate it to your magical intent.

You might like to cast a circle and invoke the Gods (see pages 62–67), then (as knives correspond to the element of air) hold your athame in the incense smoke until it is completely enveloped. Ask for the virtues of air and the blessing of the Goddess and the God to be granted to the athame. You may also want to dedicate your blade to your work as a witch. You can consecrate all of your tools in this way, if you wish, making sure that each tool is consecrated with the appropriate element.

THE WAND

The wand fulfils a similar role to the athame in that it is used for directing energy. It is often used to help witches come into contact with the green world of plant spirits. Another

masculine tool, the wand is associated with the element of fire and can also be used to invoke solar deities.

THE CUP OR CAULDRON

This tool is one of the most versatile and the most used. Its symbolism conveys the ideas of containment, blending, creation and change.

Wiccans use a cup or chalice on the altar in every ritual to symbolize the female role in the sexual union of the Gods. They also use a cauldron for mixing potions, holding spells or carrying the sacred flame during indoor rituals. The cup is considered a female tool and is associated with the element of water.

THE PENTACLE

The pentacle is a disc of stone, wood or metal. On it are inscribed symbols which include a pentagram (five-pointed star), the paired crescent moons of the Goddess,

the horns of the God and the three degree symbols. The pentacle acts as a shield to deflect unwanted or negative energy from the circle. It is a female tool and is associated with the element of earth.

Above
The cauldron is most often used by urban witches to carry water or a flame during their rites.

Left
This simple pentacle symbolizes the four elements of air, fire, water and earth, governed by the fifth element, spirit.

Visualization - the Source of Magic

Visualization is essential to making magic and should be viewed as a primary magical quest. Almost anyone can visualize. There are always going to be some people who will hear or feel, rather than see, images and they should simply adapt the following exercises to their own individual inner sense.

The easiest way to learn is to set aside five minutes a day. If you are new to visualization you will find that holding an image in your mind for just one minute is quite hard enough. As you get better you can build up the length of the exercises until you are able to carry on for ten minutes or longer.

DAY 1

Find a comfortable position and relax. Still your mind and allow your breathing to become deep and slow. Choose a simple object − a plain pebble is fine. Look carefully at it for as long as you want, close your eyes and try to see the pebble in your mind's eye. Try to hold the image for a minute. This is hard work − you will probably find that when you are sure a minute has gone by, it has only been about twenty seconds or so.

DAY 2

Repeat the same exercise with the same object, but this time try to visualize not

simply the shape of the stone, but also any markings that appear on it. Try to hold the image in your mind for at least a minute.

DAY 3

Repeat the exercise with a more complex object such as a flower or leaf. Picture the colour of the flower and each of its separate petals clearly with your inner eye. If you discover that you have a natural ability for visualization, test how long you can keep an accurate image of the flower in your mind's eye.

DAYS 4—6

Continue honing your skills. Try visualizing patterns or designs. See them with your inner eye then draw the pattern as accurately as you can. Check how closely your sketch matches the original.

DAY 7

Visualize the contents of a tray. Give yourself a minute to look at the tray, then cover it with a cloth and try to memorize everything on it.

DAY 8

Visualize your desk or dressing table. See each of the objects there in relation to one another. See the colour and grain of the desk, picture all of the details on each of the objects. Try to hold the entire image, as a whole, in your mind's eye.

DAY 9

This time, imagine a limitless pool of gold or green light filling the area around your heart. This is earth energy and we have access to it at all times. This energy is limitless and it will not tire you to use it. See the light pouring down your arms and along your fingertips. Now see a stream of bright light leap from the end of your finger. In your mind's eye turn clockwise and cast the light out to form a glowing circle.

DAY 10

Today, visualize yourself in a woodland grove. Try to build in as much detail as possible – feel the grass under your feet, the warmth of the sun, the breeze against your skin. Hear the birdsong and the sound of a stream in the distance. Now see yourself in the grove and cast the circle of light as you did yesterday.

DAY 11—13

Spend this time refining your ability to see complete scenes. Try visualizing an altar laid out with candles, water, salt and an athame. If this is easy, add detail such as horns, shells and bowls of greenery and flowers.

DAY 14

If you found visualizing the altar easy, then build up walls, pillars, or moving veils of light to create a temple. Once you have perfected this skill you will be able to create appropriate groves and temples for all your magical work. You will also be using your ability to visualize in every circle you cast.

Above
Meditation brings inner peace and insight. This High Priest is opening himself to the earth energy in Cornwall.

Left
Wherever possible, try to meditate somewhere calm and tranquil. You may want to dedicate a corner of your bedroom to this use.

Casting the Circle

Indoor altar checklist

Compass (if you don't
know the orientation of
your space)
Altar cloth
Altar candles x 2
Quarter lights x 4 (blue
for east, red for south,
green for west and yellow
or brown for north)
Pentacle
Bowl of spring water
Bowl of rock salt
Athame
Wand
Bell
Plate of cakes
Chalice full of wine
Large shell or statue of
the Goddess
Set of antlers or statue of
the God
Censer (on a well-
insulated mat)
Charcoal discs and
matches
Incense
Any other equipment (this
could mean drums, gongs,
floral crowns, cords, robes,
talismans, amulets,
potions, poppets or
fithfaths and a CD
player – whatever you
need for your rite)

Right
A small domestic altar in
honour of the Egyptian
Goddess Hathor.

Every Wiccan ritual begins with 'casting the circle'. This is equally true whether the rite is held indoors, in the woods, or on a windswept beach. The point of the exercise is to create a ritual working space that exists 'outside time and place' or, as some describe it, 'between the worlds'.

Once in place, the circle acts both to contain the magical energy raised and to protect you within it. Most circles need protection from nothing more sinister than the noise of passing traffic or the unwelcome interest of night-time dog walkers. Even so, the role of the circle is to protect and to contain energy and that is what it does.

The rules for setting up the circle are pretty much the same whether indoors or out, the main difference being that if you are working in a wood or field you will not want to carry with you elaborate sets of altar tools, lights, cloths and statues. When outdoors, keep it simple, sweep with a broom fashioned out of twigs, find something natural, such as pebbles, shells or flowers, to represent the quarters and use your finger to cast the circle.

HOW BIG SHOULD THE CIRCLE BE?

Traditionally, a magic circle is nine feet (approximately 2.75m) in diameter, but you can make it as large as you need.

It is circular because that is the shape we make when we turn around with an outstretched arm. The circle is also the symbol of wholeness and completion. Remember that the larger your circle becomes, the harder it is to hold the energy together inside it, so always try to work within a manageable space. You will learn what you can control with practice.

SETTING UP THE ALTAR

Before you begin casting your circle, you need to make absolutely sure you have everything you need, set up and ready to go. If you get half way through a rite and realize that you have forgotten an essential tool, the energy of the ritual will be dissipated and your intent may fail. Plan well ahead and make a checklist of what you need.

LAYING OUT THE ALTAR AND QUARTERS

In several Wiccan traditions, the altar is placed in the north and covered with a black, or appropriately coloured, cloth. You could use a small table or upturned box. One altar candle is placed on each side of the altar.

The Horns of the God are placed at the back of the altar in the centre and immediately in front of these are the shell or statue representing the Goddess. The pentacle is placed at the very front of the altar, again in the centre, with the bowl of water resting on it and the bowl of salt to the right. Around these objects are fitted the wand, bell, incense burner and the athames of those taking part in the rite. Athames are traditionally placed on the altar pointing north.

An appropriately coloured candle or lantern is lit at each of the quarters. This is where your compass comes in handy, if you don't already know in which direction the quarters lie.

Using a consecrated broomstick, sweep deosil (or sunwise) around the perimeter of the circle, starting in the east. The purpose of sweeping is twofold. It is useful on a practical level, particularly if you are working outside, to clear your space of any sharp twigs. On a magical level, it is an opportunity to send out cleansing energy into the space in which you will work.

ASPERGING, CENSING AND CASTING THE CIRCLE

There are traditional words for all the tasks involved in casting a circle and they have been published many times. However, as they are supposed to be spoken only by initiates, here are some alternatives, which work in the same way.

Place the point of your athame in the water. Visualize your energy flowing down the blade and filling the water with a cleansing light. You could say:

> *'By the power of the Lady and the Lord, may this water be cleansed of any negative influences.'*

Tip a little of the salt into the water, stir it and, with the tip of your athame, draw an earth-invoking pentagram (see pages 53–54) on the surface of the water. Then say:

> *'A blessing be upon this salt, may its power drive out all ill and allow in only good.'*

Take the bowl of water and consecrate yourself by sprinkling a little water over your heart.

Next, carry the bowl of water deosil around the circle and asperge (sprinkle) a ring of salt water at its perimeter.

Consecrate yourself with incense. This can be wafted or gently blown over your body.

Carry the incense deosil around the perimeter of the circle.

Using the athame, focus your attention on directing energy to the very edge of your circle. As you walk deosil around the perimeter you could say:

> *'This is the night, this is the hour*
> *Circle contain and circle protect*
> *I raise the power, I bind the power*
> *Circle contain and circle protect!*
> *In the name of Maiden, Mother and Crone*
> *In the name of the mighty Horned One*
> *I bind the power, I raise the power,*
> *Circle contain and circle protect!'*

Visualize the circle of light extending from your blade and widening to form a huge glowing sphere, which contains the area in which you are working.

Finally, carry an altar candle around the circle deosil.

Above
Some witches imagine bright flashes of cleansing energy sparking from the broom as they sweep.

Rune. This was written by Doreen
Valiente and has been reproduced in
many books and articles and is also now
on the internet. You can create your own
chant with specific meaning for you, or
you could use the one below. Whichever
form of energy raising you use, the tempo
should build steadily, getting faster until
the energy is released into the circle with
a great whoosh.

'By starlight and by pale moonlight
I dance the spiral through the night
Round the silver circle go
East and west and to and fro
South and north and back and forth
Cleanse with water, guard with earth
Light the flame and see it flair
Lift the incense to the air
Call the Old Ones in the night
Horned One and Goddess bright
By all their powers and all their might
To lend their will to this my rite.'

Once the circle is in place, the quarters
are opened. Starting in the east, welcome
the guardians of that quarter. It is
traditional to say something like:

'You mighty powers of the east
(south, west, north).
Great powers of air (fire, water, earth)
I summon, stir and call you up
To guard this circle and witness this rite
And I bid you hail and welcome!'

As you welcome the guardians, make
the appropriate invoking pentagram in the
air (see pages 46–53). Some Wiccans also
visualize the guardians or gatekeepers of
each of the quarters.

RAISING THE CONE OF POWER
With the circle established and the
quarters opened, the solitary witch then
raises the magical power that will be used
to call on the Gods or to perform any
magical work. Energy raising can take
many forms, such as dancing, chanting
or drumming. Witches following the
Gardnerian tradition chant the Witch's

When the circle is properly opened and
filled with energy most Wiccans invoke
the Goddess and the God. This may take
various forms but the most common is
the calling down of power into a
representation of the Gods such as a
statue, a pair of antlers or a shell. It
may also involve a priest or priestess
inviting the Gods to enter their bodies.
This is an extremely powerful process
and not one to be attempted by those
who are new to Wicca.

If you are starting out as a solo
practitioner don't be tempted to try this
at home. Without training you will not
know how to open yourself to the Gods,
or how to handle the energy if you
should somehow succeed. You could end
up feeling both frustrated and rather
unwell. By far the best policy is to invite
the Gods to make their presence known
in the circle and to ask them to lend their
energy to the magical work you do.

Working in the Circle

CAKES AND WINE

After the work, it is traditional to bless the 'cakes and wine' (or bread and beer or fruit and eau-de-vie, as long as the liquid is alive, i.e. alcoholic, and the food represents the fruit of the harvest). When blessing the cakes you could say:

'May the blessings of the Goddess and the God fill this food with light and life and love. May all who eat it be filled with the same.'

When blessing the wine, you could say:

'As the Grail calls the Lance, the Chalice calls the Sword and woman calls to man. Joined together they bring blessings, joy and peace.'

MAGICAL WORK

Magical work isn't easy, although it is sometimes completed very quickly. It is referred to as 'work' because it takes an enormous amount of focused concentration and energy to set up. Most solo witches will only undertake a maximum of three pieces of work per esbat because to try to do more would be counterproductive. Some undertake healing work, some have a 'green' or ecology-based bias, while others will work on an ad hoc basis when and if something is needed.

Most witches would agree that magic should be a last resort and that everyday methods of achieving your ends should always be tried first. If you want to win the Lottery, for example, buy a ticket; study for your exams rather than trying to rely on magic to pass them; and join a dating agency to meet new people, before resorting to love spells.

Eat a little of the bread and drink some of the wine, keeping a quantity to offer as a libation to the Gods after the rite.

CLOSING THE QUARTERS

At the end of the rite the guardians of the elements are thanked for their presence. You could say:

'Mighty ones of the east (south, west and north) I thank you for attending this rite And before you return to your airy (fiery, watery or earthy) realms, I bid you hail and farewell!'

Each quarter is closed by casting a banishing or closing pentacle (see pages 46–53).

Sprinkle the bread and pour the wine onto the ground and give thanks for the rite.

Left

When the circle is filled with energy, the witch will invoke the presence of the Gods into her circle.

Right

Dancing, chanting and drumming are all effective ways to raise energy within the circle.

Creating Ritual

Before attempting to put together a ritual, first decide what it is you hope to achieve. There are as many reasons for undertaking a ritual as there are ways of performing the rite itself. These can range from a desire to celebrate the turning cycle of the year, to heal yourself or someone else, to approach specific Gods or to bring yourself into contact with elemental beings.

You should also be aware of the time of year, the day and the phase of the moon on which you plan to undertake your ritual. If, for example, you wanted to enhance your physical energy you would do well to choose high summer, when the power of the element of fire is at its strongest. An appropriate day for the ritual would be Sunday and a waxing moon would be most helpful when performing 'increasing magic'.

SYMBOLISM IN RITUAL

Whatever the reason for your rite, bear in mind that in any ritual you are working with symbols. Symbols enter the unconscious (or deep mind) much more readily than speech or logic can and it is in the realm of the unconscious that we have access to our own magical worlds.

So after deciding exactly what you want your ritual to do, you should ask yourself how you can then reflect your intent, symbolically, with objects, words and actions. In their Lammas rituals, for example, many Wiccans place grain and a sickle on their altars. The grain symbolizes the power of the God, the masculine principle, which invigorates and gives us strength. As a God-symbol, grain works perfectly. The seed lies dormant in the ground during winter when the God is seen to retreat into the underworld. It grows fresh and green in early summer when the power of the sun and the power of the God are both gaining in strength. At maturity, both the grain and the God

are cut down to ensure future prosperity, as seed for the following year's harvest.

The sickle represents the Goddess' power in her 'Life in Death' aspect. In the midst of the summer, when the grain has come to fruition it is, like the God, mown down. Using the crescent-moon-shaped blade, the Goddess reaps both the harvest and the life force of the God, ensuring that the cycle of death and rebirth continues. When you choose your ritual tools or objects, try to ensure that they resonate with what you hope to achieve.

ENCHANTMENT

Wiccans use the voice, both in invocations and chanting, to reinforce the energy of their rituals. Charms and enchantment, two of the traditional skills of the witch, both take their power from the spoken word. Charms were originally prayers or incantations, which were sung during ritual to achieve a magical end, while to enchant someone meant precisely that: to chant them under your power.

Give careful thought to the words you choose in your invocations or chants. Try to make sure that they reflect, clearly, your magical intent. Remember that in the past a name was considered to hold enormous power. Do not underestimate the value of simply calling out the name of the deity or being you hope to contact, or of stating aloud your ritual's desired outcome.

Next consider how the actions you perform in your ritual will enhance the rite's symbolism. Many Wiccan rituals involve the lighting of candles or bonfires. The creation of a sacred flame, with its powers of energy, life force and illumination, is one of the most powerful acts you can perform in a ritual. In the same way, during rituals of cleansing, you may actually want to wash objects or individuals, or to asperge (sprinkle) them symbolically with consecrated water.

Left
In ritual, an action as simple as using an elemental banner to open the appropriate quarter can lend a deeper significance to your rites.

Opening	Circle casting and quarters
Power-raising/ contacting the deities	Invocation, chanting and drumming
The work (your intent)	Spellcraft
Cakes and wine	Blessings
Closing	Closing the circle down

Within this structure, rites usually contain ritualized movements, such as sweeping, consecration and circle casting, ritualized speech, such as chanting or invoking, and ritualized sensations, such as the softness of candlelight or the scent of incense. Because all of these components are formalized and repeated in every rite, the mind comes to expect them and to associate them specifically with magical work. They become triggers that stimulate the unconscious mind and help to intensify the power of the symbols being used in the rite.

When planning a rite, think it through logically from beginning to end and decide how you can make it more meaningful. Each part should contribute to the whole. Be careful not to include too many extras and complicated embellishments because you think they will add drama to the proceedings – only put in what is absolutely essential to make the ritual work.

If, for example, you wanted to hold a ritual to bring you into contact with the element of air, you would need to ask a series of questions.

Why hold the ritual? To inspire myself, and to enliven my intellect.

When to hold it? In spring, on a Wednesday, during the waxing moon.

Where to hold the ritual? An 'airy' place, if possible, such as a hillside.

Above
Witches find working with nature a renewable source of inspiration for creating their rituals.

Most rituals work best if they stick to an established formula. The less the conscious brain has to think about, the more the unconscious mind can get on with its work. The formula that most Wiccans use is generally:

If robed, what should I wear? Pale blue or yellow robes of a light material (muslin or silk).

How to open the rite? Make incense, which activates the 'airy' part of each of the elements, and cense each of the quarters.

How to raise power? Ritual chanting (because air resonates within the body).

Which Gods should I invoke? Gods and Goddesses of air/communication/learning.

What should the work involve? Making magic that will activate the intellect or inspire those present. It should include an inward breath for inspiration and a final outward breath to release the intent into the universe.

How should I close? Cense again.

What should I include in my feast? Food and drink that activates the mind and which is light and airy. You could try a salad of fresh mint and sage, steamed fish (if you are not vegetarian) – well-known as 'food for the brain' – and a lavender soufflé, all of which are known to enliven the intellect.

The final thing to remember when putting together a ritual is that it should blend together well. It is not a good idea to start with an Egyptian prayer, for example, then skip over to invoke one Celtic and one Norse deity and finish with some Greek ritual dancing. Unless you are very skilled at creating ritual, what you produce will seem muddled and confusing rather than positive and innovative. Once again, the best solution is to keep it simple. This will help you to visualize consistently.

Keep in mind that the point of any ritual is to help you achieve a state where you are in harmony with the universe. The profound symbols of the circle, the square (formed by the quarters) and the triangle (or cone of power) combine to reinforce your place in the web of creation. Every tool you use in your ritual re-establishes your connection with the elements.

Every time you invoke the Gods you are sustaining your relationship with the divine, while reaffirming the creative, polar tension between male and female.

Below
No matter how elaborate the altar or the rite, all Wiccan rituals begin with the cleansing of the working space.

Spellcraft

There are plenty of books on the market that give 'recipes' for spells – spells for wealth, spells to find love and spells to pass exams. Most Wiccans find them pretty amusing. That's not to say witches don't cast spells, of course they do, but the thing that most of these 'recipe' books fail to mention is magical intention.

Intent is a forceful expression of your magical will, your desire to make change occur. It is the one piece of magical information that is taught to every Western child by its parents and the only one that is re-enforced every year. At each birthday, candles are lit on a cake, the child is told to blow the candles out, to 'make a wish' and, if they want the wish to come true, to keep it a secret. The birthday cake is the simplest form of spell – light a candle, send out your intent and keep silent about it.

Frankly, it doesn't matter how many times you sprinkle the right number of caraway seeds into a cauldron or how many love potions you drink by the light of the waxing moon, magic will not happen without intent. You have to use your personal energy.

If you cast a spell to attract new love into your life and then spend every night slumped in front of the television you can't expect success. You have to create the right environment for the spell to work. This kind of spell will be much more likely to get a result if you put your personal power into it as well. This would mean making an effort to be sociable, going out and meeting new people – using your own power to change your life.

CREATING SPELLS

When it comes to spells I would always suggest creating your own. They will be unique to you and, as a result, much more meaningful and more likely to succeed. Before deciding what your spell 'recipe' should contain, consider whether you need a spell at all. Some things just don't need magic – they may need you to work hard, or change your lifestyle or focus clearly on a problem, but that is well within the realm of the everyday world. You must decide if magic is really the appropriate way of reacting to a given situation. If, for example, you have an accident and cut yourself, you should get a bandage on the wound, not cast a spell to stop the bleeding.

Don't rush to use magic in a frivolous way because it is likely that you will be disappointed. Before casting any spell, ask yourself: 'Do I really need to involve the great powers of the universe?'

Having decided you do need to cast a spell, the next job is to decide exactly what you want the spell to do. Be precise about what you need and be concise. Make your aim as short and clearly stated as possible. Saying something vague like 'I've got a job interview coming up and I'm not sure if I want the job, but I'd like them to offer it to me anyway' is not a

Below
Offerings of corn dollies and feather fetishes have been added to a traditional 'clootie tree' where rags are tied to branches in honour of the Gods.

useful starting point. If your magic is
going to succeed you have to want the
end result with every fibre of your being.

Writing things down is a very useful
way of cutting out extraneous ideas. Be
clear about what you want and about
why you want it. You can then have fun
deciding which sort of spell you want to
try, from cord or candle magic to potions
or poppets. You also have to decide on
which day and in which phase of the
moon to cast the spell, the appropriate
herbs, oils, crystals and candle colour to
use and, finally, which of the elemental
energies to invoke.

You can use your notes to put together
a short chant, or rhyme. Many Wiccans
find that rhyming spells work best. They
are easier to memorize and the rhythm of
the rhyme gives the spell a built-in energy.

CORRESPONDENCES

What you put in your spell is up to you,
but, if you are a beginner, it's worth
consulting a table of correspondences so
that all your components work together.
If, for example, you want to cast a spell for
the physical energy to complete a project,
aim to use the passionate force of fire and
its corresponding herbs and crystals. If you
want intellectual clarity, then the power of
air would be most useful. If, on the other
hand, you wanted to plan and carry out a
project methodically, the element of earth
would be the best choice to supply you
with patience and thoroughness.

THE ETHICS OF SPELL CASTING

All Wiccans work their magic under the proviso of the Wiccan Rede that states: 'An it harm none, do what you will.' It is considered unacceptable for any Wiccan to attempt to affect another person's free will. It doesn't matter how much you love a particular person, or how much you believe you are meant to be together, or how sure you are that they will eventually understand that you are 'the one', you should not attempt to persuade them to love you using magical means. This kind of magic sometimes does work, but neither you, nor the person on whom you have forced your will, are likely to be happy. The spell will inevitably unravel, probably in a painful, messy way, because you have not considered whether your actions are going to hurt another.

That is not to say that you can never try to find love, but you must approach magic carefully. It would be far more useful (and healthy) to cast a spell that gave you the confidence to meet new people or to take up new interests, putting you in a better position to attract love to you.

HEALING AND CURSING

Surprisingly, many new witches also make mistakes when it comes to healing work, and jump in to perform magic uninvited. 'But surely I'm doing good?' they say. 'Healing someone can't have a bad effect.' However, none of us can ever be sure of the effect our interfering will have. Unless someone specifically asks you for help with healing, do not be so arrogant as to presume to act on their behalf.

If you act without being invited to do so, you are taking away that person's free will to decide how they will approach their illness. Each individual addresses illness in his or her own way. Some people need to go through a process of coming to terms with ill health before they can start to heal. Some people will simply not

get better. It is not up to us to meddle in that process uninvited. Everybody makes mistakes, even the most experienced witches, but you will radically reduce the number of your mistakes if you always think before you act.

Finally, most Wiccans would not consider casually hexing or cursing someone. Quite apart from anything else, doing this wastes an enormous amount of personal energy. Keeping up the level of hatred and anger needed to make a curse work is extremely tiring. Worse than that, it ties you to the object of your curse. You will find that you have to keep remembering why you wanted to hurt them in the first place and that means keeping your wounds open. Cursing someone is harmful to you, because you have to keep using your own energy to maintain the spell and this stops you from healing and getting on with your life.

PROTECTION

If someone is seriously trying to harm you, either physically or emotionally, it is much more useful to act through ordinary, everyday channels. Get yourself away from them and, depending on the situation, report them to the police or social services, or to your parents or teachers. Do not allow yourself to become a victim.

If the situation is really desperate and you feel that ordinary channels are not enough, you could consider placing a binding spell on the person as a last resort. This is not a curse and does not interfere with their free will. They are still completely free to feel and to act however they like toward you – what a binding spell will do is to stop any of these thoughts, feelings or actions from harming you in any way. Many Wiccans would shield themselves by concocting a reflecting spell in which all of the ill will was bounced back to the person generating it.

Left

Spells can transform your life, provided that your intent is clear and that you support your magical work with your personal energy.

Herbcraft

Wiccans use the magical power of plants in every ritual. We burn plant resins and oils in our incense as an offering to our Gods. We anoint each other during our rites with plant oils and we celebrate the union of the Goddess and the God with cakes and wine. Both cakes and wine are derived directly from plant sources (wheat and grapes) and both are produced through the transformative action of living yeast.

Plant symbolism features throughout the festivals of the Wiccan year. As the seasons turn and plants sprout, grow and are cut down, they are seen as metaphors for the stages in our own lives. As the seed germinates in the soil, so we are carried, both in our earthly mother's womb and in the womb of the Great Goddess.

As plants grow to maturity and produce a harvest, so our own lives will produce a harvest of knowledge and experience. Finally, at death, we are laid below the ground. In the same way, the plant lies dormant through the winter but is reborn in spring, just as we are reborn in each successive generation.

Plants teach us persistence, industry and patience. They are creatures of enormous strength, as anyone who has seen a weed grow through four inches of concrete knows well. Plants are also extremely resilient and will grow and thrive anywhere – from the fourth-floor ledge of a derelict factory window to a pile of clinker beside a railway cutting.

Plants transform light into food and, as a by-product, produce the oxygen that we need to live – they are fundamental to our lives and to our well-being. The green of their chlorophyll is the second most common colour on our planet and we find the limitless tones and shades of their foliage blissfully restful. The blues, oranges and reds in plants' fruit or flowers also act to soothe, uplift or enliven us.

Many Wiccans use magical herbs in healing and to create incense, talismans, amulets, potions, ritual baths, infusions, sachets and unguents. Those with a particular affinity for the 'green world' will also seek to understand the deeper magical energies of plants.

THE GREEN PATH

To communicate with the 'green world' you have to find a deep, inner stillness within. Approach a plant that you are drawn to, or one for which you feel a particular kinship. Sit in front of it and allow your mind to become unfocused. Let your thoughts drift out toward the plant. Don't deliberately try to force your consciousness on it, but allow the energy of the plant to reach out to you. If you are unsuccessful, persevere; try the exercise every day for a month or approach a different plant or a different species.

If the plant does allow you to make contact, you will probably be amazed at the speed with which connections take place when in the green realm. You may become aware of a web of silver strands of light connecting everything in the plant world. You may find yourself transported instantly to the heart of the plant, to its very cell structure, where you may be given its true name.

Those who continue to work with the green world may also discover plant guides. These plant spirits (some call them devas) are open to communication with our world and can teach us much about the healing and magical properties of plants. Over time you may discover your own 'plant guide', a plant with which you feel you have made connections that exist on a deep ancestral or personal level.

Above

Witches revere elder all year for its seasonal harvests: flowers for cordials in early summer, berries for wine in autumn and bark and roots for salves, dyes and inks in winter.

Right

Opening yourself to the spirit of an elder allows access to the powers of the Crone: death, transformation and rebirth.

Practical Herbcraft

Above

Most witches make it a priority to learn the healing properties of simple wild flowers such as foxgloves, campion, valerian and Herb Robert.

INCENSE

Making your own incense will always produce something with much more significance and impact than a 'ready-made' product from a shop. Apart from resins and gums such as frankincense, myrrh, benzoin, copal and damar, which have to be imported, the herbs included will have been grown by you, or picked on the appropriate day and at the right phase of the moon. Each of your incenses will be unique to you and will be made with a particular purpose in mind.

A good rule of thumb is to include two to three parts resin to one part dry herbs. If you create an incense that is only made up of leaves, bark and dried flowers it will blaze away instantly and will probably just smell like burning paper. Try to include a fairly high proportion of resin, moisten dried flowers and leaves with essential oils, and finally stir in a tiny amount of oil, wine or honey, to keep the incense from burning too quickly. Store your incense in a dark, airtight jar and always write down the blend so that you can re-create it. Burn your incense on charcoal disks in an insulated censer. See the resources section for a basic esbat recipe.

ESSENTIAL OILS

If you become really enthusiastic about working with plants you may want to try making your own essential oils. It is a fairly simple process, but you need a large quantity of plant material before you begin.

In Britain it is not actually illegal to pick leaves, flowers, fruit or berries from the wild provided you do not endanger an individual plant by over-picking. You may not uproot and take home a wild plant, although you may harvest some of the roots on site. Check, carefully, the list of protected plants for your country and leave them completely alone. In the UK this list is available in the Conservation of Wild Creatures and Wild Plants Act of 1975. For lists of endangered plants in America, Europe and Australia, try looking on the following web sites:

America and Europe:
http://eelink.net/EndSpp/international-global.html
Australia:
http://www.anbg.gov.au/anpc/threats.html

The easiest essential oils to extract are those that are present in great quantities in the plant. Rosemary, marjoram or lavender oils, for example, are all easy to make at home.

You will need a large enamel (not metal, non-electric) kettle, some plastic tubing (wine-making tubing is perfect), a big bowl of ice, a jug and a pipette. First attach your plastic tube to the spout of the kettle and fix in place with tape. Fill the kettle with as much fresh herb material as you can pack in. Top up with spring water. Place the kettle on a gentle heat and, while heating, feed the pipe down through the bowl of ice (placed on a stool next to the stove) and into the jug (placed on the floor). As the kettle simmers, distilled water carrying the essential oil will drip slowly into the jug, producing scented herb or flower water which is excellent for making potions or for consecrating tools or circles. A very thin film of essential oil will float on top of the herb water. Suck this up with a pipette and store in a small, dark jar.

POTIONS (INFUSIONS, DECOCTIONS AND TINCTURES)

Infusions are made simply by placing a herb in hot water and leaving it to stand for about ten minutes – the proportions are usually 25g/1oz to 570ml/1 pint, or 5ml/1 teaspoon to a cup. This process is suitable for fresh and dried flowers and leaves. Infusions can be drunk as herbal teas, or used as compresses or baths. Ritual baths are infusions on a grand scale.

A decoction is made by boiling plant material for approximately 10–15 minutes. This process is most suitable for tough fibres such as bark, roots and berries.

A tincture is made by filling a jar with fresh or dried herbs and topping it up with alcohol (vodka or brandy are the best choices). The jar is sealed and placed in a warm spot. It is shaken gently every day for about a fortnight (usually from the new to the full moon). When ready it is strained and stored in a dark bottle.

Approximately 10 drops of tincture are added to a glass of water. The same process can be used to create infused oils for massage or anointing.

HERB SACHETS

Dried leaves, berries, roots, bark and fruit can be added, in any combination, to small paper or cloth sachets. These can be used to create protective amulets, good luck talismans or personal 'fetishes', 'mojos' or 'gris gris' for contacting individual plant spirits.

HERB CANDLES

Making candles is really easy. You simply buy a mould and some wicks and pour melted beeswax into the mould. You can incorporate fresh and dried herbs and oils into the wax while it is still liquid. These will release their essence as the candle burns.

Below
Home-made essential oils should be stored in small, dark bottles to preserve the intensity of their scent.

The Wisdom of Trees

Many religions have, as their central motif, the image known as the World Tree. In Norse mythology this tree is known as Yggdrasil, the axis of the world. Yggdrasil holds the underworld in its branches. The middle world of our everyday reality rests around its trunk and the heavens are supported in its roots. This same world tree appears as the Buddhist Bodhi tree and as the Christian Tree of Knowledge. In the esoteric Jewish tradition, the Qabalah features the Tree of Life, its branches hung with the sephiroth, or virtues, of the divine.

The tree draws its power from the earth. Its leaves fall to the ground each winter in a symbolic death, but new leaves reappear in spring, signalling regeneration. Mankind undergoes the same process of death and rebirth. Many religious systems see divine, regenerative energy as coming from above, rather than below. As a result, the world tree is often shown upside down, with its roots in the heavens, drawing down divine energy to man.

Within our own bodies there are numerous tree-like structures, the branching capillaries of the circulatory system, the twiggy branches of the respiratory system and most important of all, the trunk and branches of the nervous system, which contain dendrite (tree-like) cells, essential for communication.

Like plants, trees are great keepers of wisdom and Wiccans try to contact and share this green knowledge whenever they can. You should approach trees in the same way as plants, but as they are larger and less prone to damage it is possible to come into much closer physical contact with them. They will support us – we can climb into them and lie along the branches or relax with our backs to their trunks.

When you have made contact with a tree, lie back against it. Notice how your mood or your breathing alters as you adjust to its energy field. You may find with a tree such as a fir, or pine, that your metabolism speeds up and you feel open and energized. With a large oak or beech you may find your heartbeat slowing and your breathing becoming more regular. With a birch you may be filled with a feeling of being blessed. Each tree offers you different gifts. You could also explore chanting to an individual tree. Try different tones and pitches until you find one that resonates well. Spend a little time in aural/oral communication with the tree.

AS ABOVE, SO BELOW

One exercise that every Wiccan should try, preferably in spring while the moon is waxing, is to put an ear close up against the trunk of a tree. Choose one with a smooth skin such as beech and get your ear as close as possible to the trunk. You will clearly hear the great, green pulse of the tree pumping sap from the roots to the canopy. Try the same exercise with young and mature trees and notice the difference in their rhythms.

Left
Strong and supportive, oak trees allow us access to the vital energy of the God.

Above
Birch is associated with the purifying and fertilizing power of flame.

Divination

Wiccans use various forms of divination to look into the past and future throughout the year and most choose a system that appeals to them emotionally and intuitively. Some prefer the Nordic system of casting runes, others choose the deep, pictorial symbolism of the tarot, while others prefer the immediate approach of scrying. Many Wiccans also read palms, cast astrological charts, read tea leaves or study numerology, dowsing or pyromancy.

RUNES

Runes are steeped in the mystery of Norse mythology. The Great Father God Odin is said to have won their secret after sacrificing himself and hanging upside down for nine days and nights on Yggdrasil, the World Tree.

Runes are used for divination and, because each of the runes is a letter, they are also useful as a magical alphabet. Many witches inscribe magical words, names or sigils on runic amulets, on tools and on talismans. These can be used in spells or worn next to the body. Individual runes can also be used as a meditation tool.

TAROT

The tarot is a system involving a series of 22 picture (or trump) cards and 56 suit cards. Known as the Major and Minor arcana respectively, these are decorated with symbols taken from mythology, alchemy, religion and folk traditions.

The origins of the tarot are unknown but the first 'official' pack was recorded in the fifteenth century in Italy and was used in a complicated card game similar to bridge. Over the years the tarot evolved from a series of luxurious gilded playing cards to sets of printed paper cards used for fortune telling.

In a tarot spread the cards are laid out in patterns that indicate the past, present and future of the questioner. There are nearly two hundred tarot packs available but the beginner should start by learning on a traditional pack such as the Marseilles.

SCRYING

Scrying is another word for divination and is traditionally used when witches look into clear, shiny surfaces such as dark mirrors, crystal balls or cauldrons of water.

ASTROLOGY

Western Astrology dates back to about 4000 BCE and was developed by the ancient Mesopotamians from their astronomical systems and calendars. The Mesopotamians originally worshipped the planets but over time began to use their movements through the heavens for the purposes of prediction.

There are twelve constellations in the zodiac (Aries, Taurus, Gemini, Cancer, Leo, Virgo, Libra, Scorpio, Sagittarius, Capricorn, Aquarius and Pisces) through which the sun moves over the course of a year. The relationship between the sun, moon and planets as they move around the earth are interpreted to tell the future.

DIVINING OR DOWSING

This is one of the oldest methods of finding water, tracking down lost objects and discovering what the future holds. It simply involves holding a pendulum, allowing the weight to swing and then interpreting the answer from the direction of the swing. Dowsing for water is more commonly done with a split hazel twig or with copper dowsing rods, held loosely. When the twig starts to leap, or the rods come together, water is often underfoot.

Not every form of fortune telling appeals to everyone; the best plan is to test out a few and see whether you have a natural aptitude. If you are already drawn to a particular form of divination, practise it until you become proficient.

Right

Used in meditation, cards such as Justice, Death and The World can lead to discoveries on the themes of balance, completion and fulfilment.

Below

The traditional Celtic Cross spread is one of the most commonly used in tarot readings. It allows the reader to examine a variety of influences from the past, present and future.

Rune Magic

CASTING THE RUNES

Even if you do not consider yourself to be 'artistic' you should try to make your own set of runes, rather than buying them. Traditionally runes were carved on discs of wood and the symbols were then painted on, using the carver's blood. While painting, the power of the rune was 'sung' into each disc.

It is also possible to make a set of runes using flat pebbles. If you are too squeamish to use your own blood, try a mixture called 'Earth's Blood'. This is made by combining haematite (iron ore) powder with oil to produce a dark red, sticky pigment. Chant the name of the rune on a long continuous breath as you paint. Cast the runes individually or in threes, to see past, present and future.

THE THREE AETTIRS

There are 24 runes, divided into three aettirs (or eights). The first aett belongs to Frey, the Norse fertility God, and these runes describe the essential parts of life.

Fehu: Embodies the idea of wealth, ability to care for those you love, protection of that which you value.
Uruz: The symbol of the ancient aurochs or giant ox, Uruz symbolizes strength and courage.

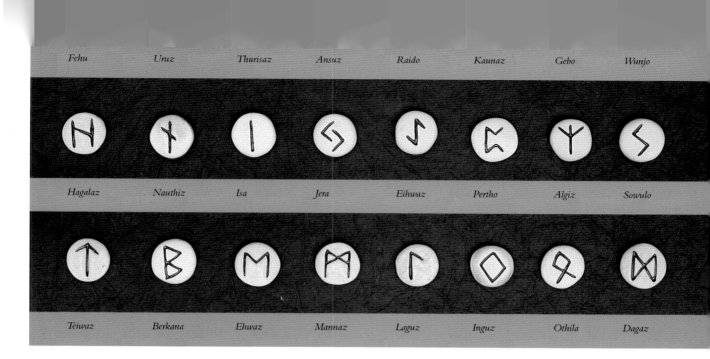

Fehu	Uruz	Thurisaz	Ansuz	Raido	Kaunaz	Gebo	Wunjo

Hagalaz	Nauthiz	Isa	Jera	Eihwaz	Pertho	Algiz	Sowulo

Teiwaz	Berkana	Ehwaz	Mannaz	Laguz	Inguz	Othila	Dagaz

Thurisaz: Violent change, often signalling problems or illness.

Ansuz: Blessings, intellectual ability, the gift of communication and authority.

Raido: Journeys, both physical and emotional.

Kaunaz: Flame of passion and illuminating light of knowledge. The ability to shed new light on a situation.

Gebo: Gifts, possibly also love.

Wunjo: Fulfilment, companionship, counting your blessings.

The second aett is Haegl's (meaning hail) and these runes symbolize the forces over which we have no control.

Hagalaz: Hail, destructive force. Lack of control.

Nauthiz: Need, both material and emotional. This rune shows that we should reassess and rethink priorities.

Isa: Ice, resistance to change, delays. The need for stability.

Jera: The end of one cycle and the beginning of another.

Eihwaz: Endurance in the face of difficulties. Links to ancestors.

Pertho: Psychic power, the workings of fate, creativity and birth, both of ideas and babies.

Algiz: Protection and defence.

Sowulo: The energy and power of the sun. Warmth and optimism.

The third aett belongs to Tyr, the God of war and of justice. These last eight runes show the human condition.

Teiwaz: Bravery and encouragement in the face of battle or competition.

Berkana: Birth, of both ideas and children. Nurturing, gestation and the ability to grow.

Ehwaz: Travel and important partnerships, friendship and co-operation.

Mannaz: How we are seen in the world, relationship with society, cycles of behaviour.

Laguz: Spiritual and physical cleansing, female power, imagination and creativity.

Inguz: Germination, human fertility, embarking on successful projects.

Othila: Inheritance, both financial and cultural. Links between generations, connection with the ancestors.

Dagaz: Sunrise, new beginnings, enlightenment.

Above

The three aettirs of Frey, Haegl and Tyr show the essence of existence, the exterior forces that we cannot control and finally our most human qualities.

Left

This priestess has chosen at random runes that signify ancestors, blessings and cycles of completion.

Chapter 3
ATTUNING TO
THE SEASONS

Before taking a decision about whether to make a long-term commitment, most 'would-be Wiccans' spend a year and a day learning about Wicca. During this magical period they try to attune themselves to the changing seasons and to the land on which they live. They celebrate, in their own fashion (usually in solo ritual), the shifting tides and energies of the year. Finally they practise meditation and establish a relationship with the great powers of the elements and with the Goddess and the God.

If you plan to celebrate the eight major sabbats and the 13 full moon esbats in the year, you will be undertaking a ritual about every three weeks. This means that each month you will have the opportunity to reassess your position in relation to the changing seasons, to rebalance and re-attune. Every time you celebrate the turn of the year, you will be re-establishing your place within the web of creation.

Learning the rhythms and cycles of the seasons is particularly important for those who live in cities. Take time to observe the path of the moon and sun over the course of each month. Record the weather and when plants and trees come into bud and flower. Get in touch with the elements by keeping track of the wild creatures you see and hear throughout the year. Find out where you can watch birds and animals locally. City dwellers are fortunate in that the number of urban foxes is on the increase. Take time to try and spot these magical creatures.

As the year unfolds, assess how you feel at each of the major turning points. Are you energized in spring, for example, or lethargic in winter? Learn your own rhythm in relation to the inward and outward spiral of the year's energy. For women it is particularly important to assess how they feel during the waxing and waning of the moon. Pay special attention to your menstrual cycle and how it affects your emotions each month.

SACRED LANDSCAPE

Over the year you will come to see your environment as a sacred landscape populated with plants and animals that re-enforce your relationship with the Gods. Try making an elemental map of your surroundings. With your home as the central point, choose an area around it and decide how far you are prepared to walk to each point of the compass. On a local map, circle all the public land such as parks, reservoirs and gardens within that distance. Next trace on your major landmarks, including any hills, rivers and roads. Mark in the open parkland.

You can now divide your area roughly into the four quarters of north, east, south and west. In each quarter try to find a meditation spot that corresponds to that element. This could be a hill or even a tower block for east, a warm terrace or sunbathing spot for south, a lake or pond for west and a quiet wooded area for north. If you don't want to go into open areas alone, try buildings instead. A library would be an excellent choice for east, a sauna or solarium for south, swimming pools would work well for west and a workshop or craft centre for north. Choose your own sacred spots and develop a relationship with the land.

Left

All boundaries between the elements are magical places, so any coastline is a perfect spot to experience the turn of the year.

Wiccan sabbats are a joyful celebration of the ebb and flow of the year, honouring each festival with a seasonal ritual.

Magical Correspondences

Element: *Earth*

Magical Tool:
Pentacle or Shield

Compass Point: *North*

Season: *Winter*

Time: *Midnight*

Age of mankind:
Old Age

Attribute: *Sensation*

Gods and Goddesses:
The new-born solar God, or 'Child of Light'. Goddess of the dormant winter earth, or the 'Dreaming Goddess'.

Right
The Yule fire symbolizes the revitalizing energy of the returning sun.

If you want to bring the Craft of the Wise into your life, you must first bring yourself into alignment with the cycle of the seasons. Nothing ties you more closely to the rhythms of the changing year than the round of Wiccan sabbats.

While very few of us still live in farming communities where we plant and reap, or even grow vegetables in our gardens, we can still understand themes such as preparation, planting and harvest in terms of the practical and emotional aspects of our lives. You will easily be able to adapt and improve on the suggestions given here to create rituals that will have a personal meaning for you, and of course you can continue to adapt them as you experience various changes throughout your life.

The Wiccan year traditionally starts at Samhain, the beginning of winter, and if you prefer to follow tradition and celebrate Samhain as the new year you will be in good company. However, if you feel that it is more appropriate for the new year to start with the birth of the new sun and the new God at the winter solstice, you can begin at Yule and follow the year through as shown here. The choice is up to you.

YULE

Yule falls on the shortest day of the year. From this point onward the days lengthen and the sun's power increases until it reaches its peak at the midsummer solstice. In Wicca, this sabbat honours the passing of the old Solar God and celebrates the birth of the new God.

At this point the old God finally relinquishes all responsibility for the physical land and its fruitfulness. He has fulfilled his various predetermined roles, having impregnated the Goddess, ensured the fertility of the land through the spilling of his own blood and taken the Goddess into the underworld for her period of regeneration over the winter months. His role is now to rejoin and be re-assimilated by the pantheon of Father-God deities. The role of the young God is to grow stronger and to return light, life and fertility to the land.

Yule is one of the few festivals that are celebrated in many of the same ways by both pagan and Christian alike – at the bleakest time of the year we fill our homes with branches of evergreen holly, ivy and mistletoe reaffirming life in the midst of death. The Yuletide season is marked by an intense period of feasting, drinking and general jollity. Fires and candles are lit in both Christian and Wiccan homes, acknowledging the life-giving power of the returning sun or the 'Sacrificial God' embodied in the brightness of the flames.

'A Year and a Day'

Actively dedicating yourself to a 'year and a day' of practising and learning more about magic will help you enhance your skills. The physical actions of your ritual will fix its purpose in your mind, and the very fact that you are making known your aim to the universe means that your 'intent' is in place, working on a higher level to help you achieve all you can.

As Yule is one of the great turning points of the year, it is an ideal time for a ritual of purification, contemplation and preparation. It is the longest, darkest night, the time of completion and the death of the old year. It is also the night on which the Goddess gives birth to the new Sun, beginning a restoration of light, life and warmth to the land.

PREPARATION

Before Yule, spend some time meditating on concepts such as rebirth, renewal and the power of the sun.

Set up your altar as usual (see pages 62–63) and decorate it with gold candles and fresh holly, ivy and mistletoe. Place an additional large, gold candle on your altar to light during the rite.

Above
Leaping the Solstice bonfire brings luck, fertility and success for the coming year.

Take the phone off the hook and warn your friends/family that you cannot be interrupted for at least an hour. Make absolutely sure that your room is warm enough – you can become quite cold if you meditate while lying down.

Find a blanket to use especially for magical work and pick a colour that has magical significance. Try blood red for the power of the life force, or pale blue to promote your spiritual development.

Just before the rite, have a leisurely bath. Use gold candles and infuse the water with essential oils such as rosemary, which purifies and repels negativity, and frankincense, which concentrates and stills the mind. Add bay leaves and a few pine needles to the water in honour of the solar Gods. While bathing, imagine yourself filling with light.

When you feel calm, and your attention is concentrated on what you intend to do, wrap yourself in a warm robe and begin your solstice ritual.

THE RITE

Consecrate the circle and open the quarters as usual.

Lie down; allow your breathing to deepen and your mind to become quiet.

Begin the solstice pathworking meditation.

Raise the cone of power.

Take a moment to collect your thoughts and find yourself fully back in your room.

Invoke the blessings of the Goddess and the God. You could say:

'I call upon you this night,
Mighty Mother of us all
Lady of the Silver Wheel
Keeper of the Spiral Castle
Be with me tonight
Bringing love, peace and
ever-renewing life.'

Wait until you feel the presence of the Goddess and then invoke the God, saying:

'I call upon you this night, Lord of Light
You are the stag upon the hill
The standing stone and the restless stream
Return on this solstice night, reborn.
Be with me tonight and banish the darkness.'

Wait until you feel the presence of the God, and then say:

'In the presence of the Great Mother and
the Lord of Light, I share in the circle of being
and dedicate myself to learning the Craft
of the Wise.'

Light the large gold candle and carry it to each quarter, saying:

'As the new dawn signals a new year
and a new beginning
So may this light signal a new phase
in my development,
May it bring me insight (east), energy
(south), sensitivity (west), wisdom (north) and
illumination (centre).'

Return the candle to the altar.

Drink some of the wine and eat one of the cakes on the altar and meditate on the themes of insight, energy, sensitivity, wisdom and illumination.

Place your gold candle on the floor and leap the flame, taking care to ensure you do not blow the candle out.

When you are ready, bid farewell to the God and Goddess, close the quarters and leave your temple. Make an offering to the Gods of some wine and some of the cakes by pouring them onto the ground.

Burn your gold candle for a few minutes every day between now and Imbolc (1/2 February). Use the time to consolidate and reaffirm your intent to learn more about the Craft of the Wise.

The Solstice Dawn

Become aware that it is nearly midnight and that you are in a pine forest. Soft, silent snow covers every tree. The night is icy and still.

Overhead the sky is indigo, scattered with pinpoint stars and shining with the pure silver light of a crescent moon.

You begin to walk north. Walking is easy, despite the deep snow, because you are strong and powerful. As you walk, fine snowflakes begin to drift down around you, covering your footprints.

You walk through the moonlit forest, the air threaded with the scent of pine and of the cold north wind. There, for a second, between the branches, you see the golden eye of a wolf, pale coat crusted with frost, breath billowing like smoke. Somewhere behind him, louder and faster, a wild boar charges between the trees, tusks glinting, master of the forest floor.

It starts to snow more heavily and the moon is hidden by clouds. You are weary now as the cold creeps along your limbs. Each step through the deep snow becomes harder and you feel icicles beginning to form on your hair and clothes. You look around for somewhere to shelter and catch a glimpse of a colossal stag on your left. His huge antlers seem almost to be entwined with the branches of the trees and they gleam silver in the starlight. He shakes his head, turns and runs – you follow as best you can, breathless, struggling to keep up.

As you finally stagger through the trees to a clearing the stag is gone, but you see a small cave on your left and enter it. Inside, the cave is dry but very cold. In the darkness you can hear a bear, dreaming through its winter rest. Hanging from branches near the roof you notice there are small bunches of leaves and berries – holly, ivy and mistletoe, braided together with cords of red and green and gold. There is a hearth at the mouth of the cave with one large, central log.

You know it is now midnight on the longest night of the year and with shaking hands you strike a spark and set the solstice fire alight. The night is long and you pass it in front of the roaring flames, watching the living fire as it leaps and turns. Morning is slow in coming, but eventually it is time to greet the dawn.

You leave the cave to face the rising sun and find on your left the mighty stag, behind you the boar, and on your right the wolf. Together you watch as the first frail beams of the newborn sun penetrate the trees and illuminate the forest. Life, light and warmth fill your body and, laughing, you jump through the solstice flames, celebrating the return of the sun.

Yule Projects

MAKING A PENTACLE

The pentacle is the foundation and basis of magical work. It is both a shield to protect the magic circle and a symbol of the earth from which we draw our power. As winter is ruled by the element of earth, now is a good time to make a pentacle, which you can use throughout your 'year and a day' of magic.

• First draw, or trace from an existing drawing, an even-sided pentagram.
• You can use your paper template to transfer this pentagram to the centre of a circle of wood or slate or a disc of air-drying clay (such as Fimo or Das). Simply transfer the outline with pinpricks or draw around your template.
• If you want to make a traditional Wiccan pentacle, you must make sure there is a gap of approximately 5cm/2in around the pentagram.
• Mark an upright triangle above the uppermost point of the pentagram.
• Mark a downward pointing triangle above the left-hand point and an 'upside-down' pentagram above the right-hand point.
• Mark the astrological symbol for Taurus below the left-hand point and

two 'back to back' crescent moons below the right-hand point.
• Under the pentagram, between the left and right points, mark on the left an S with a diagonal line through it, and on the right a capital S.

Neither unfinished wood nor air-drying clay is waterproof, so it is a good idea to seal your pentacle with a coat of beeswax or varnish.

SALT

A small pot of salt can be found next to the pentacle on every Wiccan altar. It is one of the most commonplace minerals and yet at one time salt was essential to human survival, offering the only method of preserving meat and fish through the winter. On the altar, salt represents the protective qualities of the element of earth and during Wiccan rites it is dissolved in water. This cleanses the water and creates a fusion of the two elements.

Natural sea salt is the best choice as it is unrefined. Any kind of small container can be used to carry the salt on the altar – some witches prefer a bowl, while others have special watertight pots made of wood or stone.

Left
The pentacle symbolizes the elements of air, fire, water and earth, united by the fifth element, spirit, within the circle of the cosmos.

Right
At Yule, Wiccans create special altars in honour of the birth of the new sun. Here, amber surrounds and protects the solar candles. Holly symbolizes life in the midst of death; mistletoe brings blessings and peace.

Imbolc

Imbolc, pronounced Imolc or Imbolg, is one of the Greater Sabbats of the Wiccan year.

Magical Correspondences

Element: *Fire/water*

Magical Tool:
Chalice and wand

Compass Point:
North/east

Season: *First growth of plants*

Time: *Before dawn*

Age of mankind:
Before birth

Gods and Goddesses:
All Virgin Goddesses and flame Goddesses, such as Athena, Diana, Vesta, Brigid/Brid, The Maiden. All fire Gods such as Diancecht, Februus.

Right
At Imbolc, many witches invoke the protective fire of the Goddess Brigid to celebrate the re-awakening of the earth.

Imbolc is celebrated over 1/2 February and probably derives from early pagan fertility rites, which marked the end of winter and the very beginning of spring.

An alternative name for Imbolc was Oilmelc, which meant 'Ewe milk', and the earliest festivals seem to have been closely connected with ensuring the fertility of the flocks. In the period around Imbolc, ewes begin to lactate in preparation for lambing. This would have been cause for celebration in early communities on two levels. First, it was a welcome signal that winter was truly losing its grip on the land and second, fresh milk was a valuable commodity to those who had been struggling to survive on ever-shrinking supplies of dried stores. So important was this early milk to Celtic societies that in some instances the very action of churning milk to make butter became synonymous with fertility and prosperity.

THE VIRGIN GODDESS
Many early rituals revolved around the Goddess Brig. She was known by a variety of names across Celtic Europe including Bricta, Brigindo, Brigantia and later Brigid or Bride. Brigid symbolized strength, power and vital energy. She was a Goddess of flame and of water, whose arrival signalled the quickening of the earth after the death-like slumber of the winter months.

Both rivers and holy wells were sacred to Brigid and her name survives in many current British place names from Briddle (Brigid's Well) Springs in Wiltshire, to Bridewell in London.

Brigid was also the patron Goddess of poets, healers and smiths. In Celtic mythology she is given two sisters, a typical device that indicates that Brigid was seen as a triune Goddess embodying purity, fertility and wisdom.

Records of early Imbolc folk customs indicate that Brigid was seen primarily as a symbol of renewed fertility. In the Scottish Highlands it was traditional to create a 'Bride's Bed' on the eve of 2 February. Married women would dress a sheaf of grain and rushes in white material and decorate it with ribbons. They would create a bed from a pile of reeds and on one side would place a phallic pine-cone wand – symbol of the fertilizing power of the God.

The Bride's Bed was invariably placed next to the hearth, the symbolic centre of the home where the household fire was lit. The Goddess was then invited to enter the bed. The grain figure was laid in the bed and the women would withdraw until morning.

The next day the ashes around the hearth were closely inspected. If there was an imprint of a foot or the mark of a wand, it was believed the God had visited the Goddess during the night and a fertile and prosperous year would follow. Ancient purification rituals also involved washing in sacred wells at Imbolc. The tradition has survived in the present-day Irish custom of visiting Holy Wells on St Brigid's day and in the widespread ritual of spring cleaning.

Imbolc rituals may also have re-enacted the reawakening of the land. There are certainly accounts of communities passing through a womb-like 'Girdle of Brigid'. A rope of plaited straw was held up to form a circle while villagers were symbolically reborn by stepping through it. Women also made special Brigid's Crosses from rushes and straw. It seems likely that these crosses represented the fertilizing power of fire.

In Wicca, Imbolc marks the return of the Virgin Goddess to the land. She is seen to retreat below the earth over winter to give birth to the new God at Yule. In early spring, after a period of renewal, she returns to earth restored. As every Imbolc sees the regeneration of the Goddess, so every new spring sees the earth reborn. Brigid's arrival is traditionally marked by the visible lengthening of the days and by the first snowdrops of the year.

Welcoming Spring

PREPARATION

As Imbolc is a symbolic time of renewal and cleansing, it is a useful opportunity to rid yourself of unhelpful patterns of behaviour and to prepare yourself for the coming year.

Take the time to make a list of those things you feel do not serve your progress as a witch. You might discover, for example, that self-consciousness, lack of concentration or lethargy are getting in the way of your magical work. You may consider yourself tied to old habits, or cycles of dependence, that you no longer feel to be healthy or useful.

Seriously consider how these negative habits are affecting your life, both magically and in the everyday world. Try to imagine what you would be able to achieve without these inhibitors to

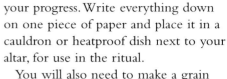

your progress. Write everything down on one piece of paper and place it in a cauldron or heatproof dish next to your altar, for use in the ritual.

You will also need to make a grain maiden to lie in Bride's Bed during the ritual. Take a bunch of reeds or dried stalks of grain and wrap them in white material. Decorate the bundle with white and green ribbons. If you do not already have one, make a phallic pine-cone wand by attaching a pine cone to the end of an oak or ash shaft. Place these, along with a green or white cloth, on the floor next to your altar.

Set up your altar in the usual way and decorate it with as many tapers and candles as you can safely include. Make sure that each candle is in a safe, stable holder. Take particular care with naked flames as this is a fire ritual and fire often has a way of making its presence felt, in a very real way. If you have a birch wand add this to the altar. If you wish you can decorate the altar with fresh snowdrops.

Before the ritual, take a bath in which you have poured a cup of sea salt and, if possible, a few drops of birch essence or essential oil. Make sure your bathroom is lit by as many candles as you can safely burn. While you bathe, concentrate on the purifying qualities of birch and salt.

THE RITE

When you feel focused, wear a white robe and begin your Imbolc ritual.

While you sweep, chant quietly:

*'Thus we banish winter
and thus we welcome spring.'*

Consecrate the circle and open the quarters in the usual way.

Lie down, allow your breathing to become slow, deep and regular. Allow your mind to become still.

Right

Wiccans often use sympathetic magic, creating circles and walkways of flame, to welcome Brigid to their Imbolc rites.

Below

As the frost retreats and the first green shoots of the year appear, we offer libations of wine to the Virgin Goddess.

Begin the Imbolc meditation pathworking.

After your meditation, take a moment to collect your thoughts until you are ready to continue.

Take your Grain Maiden and gently wrap her in the square of material. Place the phallic wand on the floor next to her. Using the tapers and candles on the altar, form a ring of flames around the Bride's Bed. Chant: 'Bride is welcome. Bride is come' until you feel the presence of the Goddess. You could say:

'Blessed Goddess, I call upon you at this feast of flame. Bestow the purifying strength of your fire and the cleansing power of your water on this rite.'

Next take the cauldron and place it before the Bride's Bed. Take the piece of paper on which you have written all those things that you wish to banish from your life. Say:

'As fire purifies and water washes clean, so may I banish the past and prepare for the future.'

Carefully light the paper from one of the candles and drop it into the cauldron. When all the paper has turned to ash, drip a little of your consecrated salt water onto the ashes.

Drink some of the wine and eat one of the cakes; as you do, meditate on the themes of purification and renewal. Save half of the cake and half a glass of wine to offer in thanks to the Gods.

When you are ready, bid farewell to the Goddess, close the quarters and leave your temple. Make sure you do not leave any naked flames unattended.

After the rite, sprinkle the cake crumbs over the grass and pour the wine onto the earth in a libation of thanks. Tip the ashes from the cauldron into running water or onto the ground.

Goddess of Flame

You are standing on a frozen lake. It is night and the pale, full moon lies low on the horizon.

The sky is violet, streaked with threads of transparent white clouds which race before the wind. The air is impossibly cold, but you are wrapped in layer upon layer of thick white wool and do not feel the crystals of ice that form in your hair.

In the distance you hear music – the thin song of a reed whistle, the high, pure note of a brass cymbal and the tinkling repetition of the sistrum. You walk across the ice, feeling the snow crush under your feet. You see musicians arriving from every direction. Some play lutes and mandolins, others violas. Others beat a fast, steady rhythm on tambours. Dancers appear, carrying flaming torches and crosses fashioned from reeds. Their green and white capes billow in the icy wind.

You join the dancers and find yourself walking more quickly through the thick snow. You pass white-furred foxes and hares darting between the feet of the crowds. Overhead you hear the low, steady rhythm of the beating wings of huge flocks of snow geese. Voices call out, 'She will come, She will come.' The front of the procession is led by two huge bears. They may be women dressed in bearskins, you cannot be sure. Between them is slung a harness in which rests a bundle of grain and reeds, wrapped in a pearl-white gown. The bear-women increase their speed – they are making their way toward a white castle. Its walls rear up out of the snow and you cannot tell if they are made of marble or of ice. The musicians quicken their pace and the dancers whirl ever

faster, their capes and torches blurring into spirals of green and gold.

The bear-women gently place the bundle of reeds in an arched room. They cover it with a veil of the finest white muslin and begin to light the many candles resting on the floor and window ledges. They create a pathway of flame. The cry of the geese overhead is joined by voices in the crowd. 'She is welcome, She is come!' they call, 'She is welcome, She is come!'

As you watch, the Goddess rises up from the candles' glow. She is shining, dazzling as flame, brilliant as starlight. She is dressed in the muslin veil and the pearl-white gown; on her brow rests a crescent moon and silver flame licks about her pale skin. 'She is welcome, She is come!' cry the geese, and the dancers whirl faster and faster.

Her smile is terrible and powerful. She opens her arms and a wave of warmth spreads out across the ice. She turns and treads a path from the archway out across the frozen landscape. Where her feet touch the ice, the frost retreats and tiny shoots of green spike upwards, opening to reveal the pale, fragile heads of the first snowdrops.

One of the bear-women speaks for the first time. She throws her arms into the air and shouts 'Thus we banish winter and thus we welcome spring.' The crowd continues to sing and to play and you walk with them back the way you came.

Imbolc Projects

RITUAL ROBE

One of the first things you will need for your year and a day of magic is a robe for meditation and ritual. A robe doesn't have to be elaborate, but it should not be worn for anything else and should signify to you that you are about to undertake magical work.

Simple robes are not hard to produce and you don't need any real sewing experience to make one. Your material needs to be about 1.5m/5ft wide and twice your height from ankle to shoulder, with a couple of spare centimetres/inches for hemming. The easiest way to create a robe is to place a doubled-over piece of material on the floor, lie down on it and get someone to draw round you with a piece of chalk. Make sure that they leave a margin of approximately 15cm/6in around your body. All you need do then is cut out the shape, sew up the sides

and cut a hole for your head to go through. It can be as easy as that, although if you're interested in sewing you can use a pattern to produce something much more sophisticated with a hood and pockets – but these are not really essential.

The most important thing when creating a robe is to use natural fibres. Don't be tempted to go for acrylic velvet or diaphanous nylon gauze. If these brush against a candle or come into contact with a bonfire flame they could catch light very quickly. Artificial fibres can also build up a nasty charge of static electricity! Choose cotton, wool or linen. Whatever your robe is made from, take care around naked flames, particularly if you choose long, flapping sleeves.

The standard witch's robe is black. This colour was originally worn so that those working outside could retreat into the darkness of the night if they were disturbed. Anyone in a hooded black robe becomes virtually invisible at night, even during the full moon. Black is also the colour of spirit and of the earth, which again makes it a highly appropriate choice. Other than black, you can pretty well choose any colour you like. White and bright green are traditional colours for Beltane, while gold and yellow can be worn at Midsummer and Lammas. It's really up to you.

BRIGID'S CROSS
To create a simple Brigid's Cross, gather a bunch of rushes of the same length and thickness (if you can't find rushes, try using sea-grass from a craft shop or even drinking straws). The rushes need to be approximately 50cm/20in long. If you want to follow tradition, you should bless the rushes and feast with them underneath the dining table before you make your cross.

1 Hold one of the rushes/straws vertically.
2 Fold a second straw in half horizontally. Slip it over the first straw at a right angle and push the fold to the centre of the first straw so that the two loose ends point to the right.
3 Hold the overlapping rushes firmly between thumb and forefinger.
4 Holding both straws in place, turn them 90 degrees anticlockwise (to the left). The two loose ends of the second straw will now be pointing upward.
5 Fold a third straw in half over both parts of the upward-pointing second straw so the loose ends of the third straw point to the right (i.e. repeat phase 2).
6 Turn again through 90 degrees anticlockwise, holding all parts firmly in place.
7 Keep folding and adding straws in this way until your Brigid's Cross is as large as you want. Remember to keep folding new straw to the right and turning the cross to the left.
8 When you are happy with your cross, tie red thread around each of the bundles of loose ends.
9 Allow your reed cross to dry thoroughly.

Above
Made fresh each spring, the Brigid's Cross can be hung in the home to bring protection and luck through the coming year. Last year's crosses are then burned in the new Imbolc fire.

The spring equinox falls around 21/22 March and marks one of only two points in the year when day and night are of equal length.

Magical Correspondences

Element: *Air*
Magical Tool:
Athame/censer of incense
Compass Point: *East*
Season: *Spring*
Time: *Dawn*
Age of mankind:
Infancy
Attribute:
Potential/thinking
Gods and Goddesses:
*Aphrodite, Eostre,
Minerva Isis,
Blodeuwudd, Adonis,
Lord of the Greenwood,
Dylan, Osiris Attis, Pan,
Faunus, Dionysus*

In Wicca this time is seen as a period of balance and of waiting potential because, from the equinox, the power of the God and of the sun begins to grow rapidly until the midsummer solstice.

In Northern Europe the equinox and the following month of April mark the traditional period of seed planting. The symbolism is explicit – the solar power of the God has warmed the cold soil of spring and the Goddess, as earth, is ready for ploughing and impregnation. Light and life have won a victory over darkness and death.

In classical Rome the ancient cult of Attis, son of the Great Goddess Cybele, began a ten-day festival in the middle of March which ended around the equinox. Attis was a more modern version of older sacrificial Gods such as Tammuz, Osiris and Dionysus. At his festival a pine tree, symbolizing the God, was cut down and wrapped in a shroud.

The tree was placed in a sepulchre and temple priests took part in ecstatic mourning dances in an attempt to revive Attis and bring him back to life. A few days later, the tomb was opened and shown to be empty. The solar Attis was seen to have descended into the wintry gloom of the grave and to have risen again, conquering the darkness.

While many Christians deny any link between the events of their Easter festival and those of the much more ancient Attis cult, it seems highly likely that the Christian Church adopted some of these earlier and very popular rites to celebrate the rebirth of their Christ. Like Attis, Christ is buried in a shroud in a dark sepulchre and, like Attis, he is seen to vanish from the tomb after a period of three days, indicating his rebirth.

THE GODDESS EOSTRE

Present-day Easter celebrations in Europe are still closely linked to the spring equinox and are an amalgam of several ancient traditions. The name Easter is derived from the festival of Eostre or Ostara, a Teutonic Goddess of the dawn. In *A Witches' Bible*, Stewart Farrar puts forward the theory that the name Eostre is a corruption of Astarte or Ishtar.

Eostre's feast was held on the first full moon after the spring equinox. It celebrated the opening of the gates of dawn and the return of light to the land. The later, Christianized, Easter was arranged to fall on the first Sunday following the full moon after the equinox.

Easter is still a movable festival, which can fall anywhere between 22 March and 25 April.

Three ancient pagan symbols, the hare, the egg and the hot cross bun, have persisted to the present day and have become incorporated into Christian Easter celebrations. The magical hare, known for its fertility and its role as companion to the Goddess Eostre, has survived and has been trivialized as the Easter 'bunny' that traditionally hops around delivering Easter eggs.

The egg is itself an ancient symbol of dormant possibility and, like the seed, contains the potential of new life. It is also a symbol of completion and wholeness. In mythology a Mother Goddess figure often lays a cosmic egg, representing the world, which is then cracked open, or brought to life, by the fertile heat of the God as sun.

The confusion over hares laying eggs is an ancient one. Some think that early peoples may simply have mistaken a bird's nest for the hare's nest-like form and believed that the hare laid eggs. There is also a legend that Eostre found an injured bird at the end of winter and, in order to save it, transformed it into a hare. The hare was then believed to retain the bird's ability to lay eggs.

The origin of the hot cross bun may be as ancient as the worship of the Babylonian Goddess Ishtar. Certainly the Babylonians, the Egyptians and the ancient Greeks and Romans all made and offered small cakes to their various moon Goddesses at the spring equinox. These were marked with crescent-like curves, which may have symbolized both the horns of the moon and the fertility of the ox (associated with Hathor and Isis). Some researchers believe the ancient Greek word boun, which meant ox, could have evolved into our present word bun. These equinox cakes became common all over Europe and were made with ingredients that reflected the change in the seasons. With the arrival of the warmer weather, cows began producing milk and hens started laying again.

Equinox buns all contained a high proportion of eggs and milk, included as sympathetic magic to ensure a good supply of both over the coming season. In time, the symbol of the horns evolved into a cross, which represented the phases of the waxing, full, waning and dark moon and the four points of the compass. When the Christian Church annexed the festival of the Goddess, the Church fathers adopted her symbols and the cross on top of the bun came to symbolize the cross of Christ.

Most Wiccans include seed planting as part of their spring equinox rites. The seed symbolizes the potential of the coming year and the act of pushing the seed into the soil echoes the impregnation of the Goddess by the young priapic God.

Below

As the year turns and the weather improves, many witches try to work outdoors as often as possible. At a meeting point of earth, air and water, they carry the makings of a bonfire to warm them during their rite.

Sowing the Seed

Above

Each egg contains the potential for new life and symbolizes both the individual and the cosmos.

PREPARATIONS

You will need to choose the seeds that you intend to plant during the rite. These will signify your magical hopes for the coming year. If, for example, you aspire to courage and joy, plant borage seeds. For purification, choose basil, fennel or rue. For closer contact with the God, plant sunflower or calendula seeds or, for a deeper understanding of the Goddess, choose Lady's mantle, hollyhock or poppy seeds. Place your seeds and a flowerpot filled with soil next to the altar.

You will need one white and one black candle for the altar. You will also need a second bowl filled with clean water.

Decorate your altar with daffodils, tulips and daisies. Yellow flowers are traditionally associated with Eostre. If you can find them, add some alder buds to the altar to symbolize the theme of rebirth.

Decorate eggs for your altar. In some countries the custom is to paint raw eggs blood red to symbolize life and renewal. In Britain eggs are usually dyed while they are being hard-boiled. To create a bright yellow dye, pick a large handful of gorse flowers and boil these in the water. Beetroot skins will produce a pale pink dye, while onion skin will dye your eggs a warm russet. If you boil white eggs with cabbage leaves and a cup of vinegar they will turn pale blue, but this colour is not fast and it rubs off easily.

While you take your ritual bath, meditate on the theme of awakening, potential and rebirth.

When you feel focused, choose a white or black robe and begin your equinox ritual.

THE RITE

Consecrate the circle and open the quarters in the usual way.

Lie down and allow your breathing to become slow, deep and regular. Allow your mind to become still.

Begin the equinox meditation pathworking.

Take a couple of minutes to compose yourself and collect your thoughts.

Raise the cone of power. Then invoke the Goddess into the circle, saying:

'At this turning point of the year, at this instant of poise, balance and potential, I welcome you Eostre, Goddess of the new dawn, to this equinox rite. Blessed Goddess, who carries the egg of the world within her, be with me now.'

When you feel the presence of the Goddess, invoke the God into the circle, saying:

'Lord of the ox and the plough, Lord of death and rebirth, be with me now, you who are protector of fold and flock, whose strength grows with every rising of the sun. Lend your power to this rite, light the fire within the womb of the Goddess.'

When you feel the presence of the God, take the pot of earth and the seeds. Place them before the altar, saying:

'May the blessing of the Goddess and the God be upon these seeds, that they may stir and quicken to life. Like my aspirations, these seeds have lain in preparedness through the long winter: like me, they are full of potential. The Lord of light has returned to the land and the Lady is ready to bring them to fruition.'

Place the seeds on the surface of the soil, saying:

'I consecrate these seeds with the element of earth, may they grow strong in substance.'

Next, carefully sprinkle a little of the sweet water (not salt water) on the seeds, saying:

'I consecrate these seeds with the element of water, may they grow in harmony.'

Next breathe over the surface of the soil, saying:

'I consecrate these seeds with the element of air, may they grow in balance.'

Finally, hold the pot of seeds toward the white candle flame, saying:

'I consecrate these seeds with the element of fire, may they grow in strength and power.'

Spend some moments visualizing your aspirations coming to fruition.

Drink some of the wine and eat one of the eggs you have decorated.

Meditate on your hopes for the coming year.

Thank the Gods and close the circle in the usual way. Make a libation to the Gods.

Below

Spring is a typical time for cleansing. Here, a priestess burns the dried poppies and grains she used in her equinox rites of the previous autumn.

Follow the Plough

Become aware that you are standing on the edge of a small wood. Behind you is a village and in front of you a large square field, ready for the plough.

It is morning and the new-washed sky is a clear, wet blue. Fat rain clouds scud through the bright spring air. You sit for a while, feeling the earth beneath you.

Early in the day it rained, but now the soil has dried in the sun and it is warm to the touch. You pick up a clod of earth and let it rest in your open hand, hot and red and full of life.

Suddenly you hear laughter and looking back toward the village you see a column of young women dancing toward you. They are carrying sticks and poles, which they are using to vault high into the air. As they reach the boundary of the field they seem to be competing to see who can jump the highest. Each leap is greeted with a roar of laughter and applause.

Behind them come the rest of the people of the village, dressed in every shade of green and brown.

At the centre of the crowd is the young queen, draped in a robe that echoes the warm ochre of the earth. The hem is woven with heads of wheat, barley and oats. She walks with a steady, proud step, her head held high. She is carrying a white candle in one hand and a black candle in the other. Behind her a team of oxen pulls a great plough. They are driven by a young warrior whose red-gold hair is blown about his brow like a halo of flame.

Leaving the crowd behind her, the young queen walks to the centre of the field. In the distance you see her shrug off her robe, which she spreads on the warm earth. You see a flicker of pale skin as she lies down upon the robe and waits for the plough.

The young warrior stirs the oxen on and they begin to plough a great sunwise furrow, spiralling toward the centre of the field and the waiting queen. The sun is rising fast and the day is warm.

The girls continue to leap and vault around the edges of the field. They shout encouragement to the warrior, urging him to plough faster. They call to him that the land is waiting for the plough, the earth for the seed.

It is midday. The sun is high overhead. The warrior reaches the centre of the field. You see him stoop and lie by the queen. You feel a shiver rush across the fields. It is done. The land is ploughed.

Now the queen and the young warrior climb onto the backs of the oxen; together they plough a widdishins spiral back to the edge of the field. On their return all of the villagers step up to the furrow and start to make their way in single file, into the centre of the field and out again. As they walk the intertwined labyrinths they scatter seed into the warm earth.

Spring Equinox Projects

THE ATHAME

Spring is the right time to think about buying an athame. This magical tool is governed by the element of air and air corresponds to spring and to new beginnings. Although it is always better to make your own tools, most witches end up having to buy their first athame. It isn't easy to find a blacksmith prepared to let you take part in the creative process and it is both complicated and tricky trying to make your own. A compromise might be to buy just the blade and to make your own hilt, or handle.

This is fairly easy to accomplish by choosing two pieces of wood of the correct size, then carving them roughly to the shape you need. Trace round the tang, which is the non-blade part of the knife, onto one half of the hilt. Very carefully carve or chisel the shape of the tang from one of the pieces of wood. The two halves of the hilt should now fit together perfectly, enclosing the tang.

Glue the tang firmly in place, glue the two halves of the hilt together and then sand and finish the hilt until it fits your hand comfortably. It is essential to glue the tang into the hilt very securely – you do not want your blade coming loose during a rite.

When the hilt is finished, either paint it black or bind it with black cord or leather, as you wish. Finally consecrate your blade and dedicate it to your magical aims.

There are notes for making your own blade in chapter 6 (see page 184).

INCENSE

The censer of incense is one of the central tools on the Wiccan altar. It is used to carry the perfumed gums, bark and resins that Wiccans use to consecrate their sacred space and which rise as offerings to the Gods. Once again, spring is a favourable time to choose a censer because, like the athame, the censer is ruled by air.

Your censer can be as elaborate or as simple as you like. Some Wiccans enjoy using a special brass censer with lots of decorative touches, while others are happy to use their cauldrons.

The most important thing is that the censer must have a well-insulated handle. You will be amazed at how much heat a tiny disc of burning charcoal can generate, and at how quickly this happens. If the handle becomes uncomfortably hot while you are busy censing, you will soon find that you are unable to concentrate on the magical energy of the job.

The last thing to remember when using a censer is to take great care when using the lid. If your censer has a metal lid (and most of them do) through which the smoke pours in beautiful swirls, don't forget that it is directly above the burning charcoal and will become very, very hot indeed. Once in place you won't be able to shift the lid until the censer cools down. If you want to add more incense to your charcoal during your rites or meditations, leave the lid off.

EQUINOCTIAL AIR INCENSE

1 part Frankincense gum
1 part Benzoin gum
1 part Colophony (pine resin)
1 part Gum Arabic (acacia)
2 parts Gorse blossom
2 parts Daisy petals
$\frac{1}{2}$ part Honey, wine, oil mix
9 drops Peppermint oil

Grind the gums and resins together and stir in the essential oil. Next blend a little honey, wine and olive oil is equal parts and add this to the mix to prevent it from burning too quickly. Store the incense in a dark, airtight container and burn on charcoal disks in a well-insulated censer.

Left
Athames can range from elaborate Egyptian, Celtic or fantasy designs to a simple blade with a black oak handle. Always make your choice based on how the athame feels.

Beltane

30 April/1 May **Beltane** Sun moves into Taurus

Beltane – from Bealtaine or Bealtuinn – marked the start of the Celtic summer and, with Samhain, was one of the two great axis points of the ancient year.

Magical Correspondences

Element: *Fire*
Magical Tool:
Chalice/wand
Compass Point:
South east
Season:
Beginning of summer
Time: *Mid morning*
Age of mankind:
Youth
Attribute:
Creativity/fertility
Gods and Goddesses
Aphrodite, Venus, Frigga, Robin Goodfellow, Puck, the Horned God, Pan.

Right
Many Beltane rites incorporate a cup or chalice which symbolizes the fertile womb of the Goddess.

The Celts saw the world in terms of light and dark, male and female, summer and winter, birth and death, growth and regeneration. Winter contained the festivals of death (Samhain) and rebirth (Imbolc) and summer celebrated growth (Beltane) and harvest (Lammas).

These feasts were linked with the herding and agricultural rhythms of early communities. Beltane ushered in samon, the light half of the year. It was traditionally the time for planting, and coincided with the period when flocks were taken to their upland pastures. The Celts made creative use of sympathetic magic, and sexual abandon was encouraged at Beltane to ensure the fertility of both flocks and harvest.

Beltane meant either the 'fire of the sun God Bel' or simply 'lucky, bright fire' and was a festival of fertility and purification. New growth required a symbolic death and a period of cleansing and regeneration. Every fire in the community was doused before the single central bonfire was rekindled using nine sacred woods. Each household then relit their hearth fires from the new Bel flame. Flocks were

driven through the sacred smoke to cleanse them on their way to pasture.

Later Beltane celebrations incorporated additions such as the maypole, gathering may and the Green Man, all variations on the theme of fertility. The maypole was usually decorated with flowers and ribbons and plunged, upright, into the receptive womb of the earth, symbolizing the union of male and female. Communities danced around the pole, weaving the ribbons to tie in the fertility of the coming year.

The first open hawthorn or may blossom signalled that the earth was warm enough to plant out crops. On the eve of 1 May, groups of youths and girls would spend the night 'a Maying' in the woods, finding blossom to decorate the maypole and forming 'greenwood marriages' (brief sexual liaisons). Any children conceived were known as Robinson or Godkin after Robin Goodfellow, the fertile spirit of the woods.

The Green Man or 'Jack in the Green' was a symbol of the regenerative power of plants, which, when cut down, spring back with renewed strength. A figure clothed in foliage was ripped to pieces by the crowd and the scattered leaves kept for good luck.

In Wicca, Beltane is perhaps the most erotic of all the sabbats. When the earth is at its most green, tender and beautiful, Wiccans honour the sacred union of God and Goddess. Like earlier generations, they jump through the Beltane fires, ensuring their own good luck for the coming year.

Union of the Gods

PREPARATIONS

As this is the most sensuous sabbat of the year, you should prepare by treating yourself indulgently. Have a massage and concentrate on the voluptuous tactile sensation of touch. Luxuriate in a warm bath filled with scented oils. Feel the water all over your body. Dress in a green robe and wear your flower or leaf crown.

Spend some time remembering your first kiss, a wild affair, or meeting the person you have loved most in your life. Feel again that rush of adrenalin and the light-headed joy of infatuation. Remember the erotic heat of passion and the tenderness of love.

Decorate your altar by creating a Beltane bower. Make an arch of lush greenery over your altar and fill your space with fresh flowers, ribbons and leaves. Choose bight green candles. Place a large bowl of earth next to the altar. Choose one large gold or yellow candle to act as your Bel flame.

Create a feast of sensual foods such as chocolate or asparagus.

Make up a Beltane cup and decorate it with flowers.

Cut hawthorn blossom in honour of the Goddess.

Below
During a Beltane celebration, Wiccans capture the fertility of the season by dancing around the maypole.

Prepare a wand of peeled oak or ash wood. If you are artistic you could carve one end into a phallus. Choose one ribbon of white and one of green.

THE RITE

Cast the circle and open the quarters in the usual way. Also light the 'Bel' candle. Lie down and allow your breathing to become slow, deep and regular. Allow your mind to become still. Begin the Beltane meditation pathworking.

Take a couple of minutes to compose yourself and collect your thoughts, then continue with the rite. Invoke the Goddess into the circle by dancing and by chanting:

'Inanna, Ishtar, Aphrodite, Godiva, Marian and Astarte.'

Continue chanting until you feel the presence of one of these Goddesses of Love and Fertility.

Invoke the energy of the God into the circle by drumming and by chanting:

*'Faunus, Tamuz, Aengus, Adonis
Faunus, Tamuz, Aengus, Adonis
Priapus, Dummuzi, Sylvanus, Dionysus!
Priapus, Dummuzi, Sylvanus, Dionysus!
Io Pan, Io Pan, Io Pan, Pan, Pan!
Io Pan, Io Pan, Io Pan, Pan, Pan!'*

Continue until you feel the energy of one of these Gods of Love or Fertility enter the circle.

Lift the golden 'Bel' candle from the altar and gently blow out the flame. Say:

'From death comes life and from darkness light. May the blessings of the Goddess and the God be upon this new Beltane flame.'

Relight the candle and jump over it three times. Carry the candle to each altar light and quarter light in turn. Blow each one of the lights out and relight it from your 'Bel' flame.

Take your phallic maypole from the altar and tie the two ribbons at the top of the wand. Wind the ribbons around the wand, crossing them back and forth. Say:

'As dark balances light and death brings forth life So the hind calls the stag, and woman calls to man.'

Take the pot of earth and push the base of the maypole firmly into the soil so that it stands upright, saying:

'Male to female, lance to grail, that is the mystery which brings everlasting joy. May the coming year be filled with delight and fertile with possibilities. So mote it be.'

Eat your aphrodisiac feast and drink some of the Beltane cup. Spend your time meditating on the themes of duality, fulfilment and sensuality.

Close your circle in the usual way.

Make a libation to the Gods.

After your rite, rise with the Mayday dawn and wash in the dew. Beltane dew is infused with the purifying power of both water and fire and is said to ensure health and prosperity for the coming year.

Above
Beltane rites often include a symbolic battle between the Oak King representing Summer and the Holly King who personifies Winter. Summer triumphs over winter and the Holly King is beaten.

Chase & Capture

Become aware that you are standing in an open clearing in an ancient forest. On either side, the trunks of aged oaks and beech trees rise up like pillars.

Silver birches sprout between them, their frail green leaves glittering in the breeze. It is just after dawn. The sun dapples down through the canopy of leaves and by the time the light reaches you it glows green.

You look down and see at your feet a carpet of primroses, orchids and bluebells. Tendrils of their sweet scent rise around you in the warm air. You see a mossy path and begin to walk forward. Off to the left you hear a woodpecker drumming against a tree and, a few seconds later, the call of the first cuckoo of the year.

As you walk, the sun grows warmer. Far away you can just hear children singing and laughing. 'For we are up as soon as any day', they sing, 'for to fetch the summer and the may!' You turn away from their voices and walk further into the forest. There is no path now and you pick your way carefully through the green.

Suddenly you notice that the birds have stopped singing. The breeze has dropped and around you everything is hushed and still. Not the call of a bird, not the footstep of a creature breaks the silence. This is the heart of the wood.

A shiver runs through you and you look quickly over your shoulder. You see nothing but your heart starts pounding. You are sure there is something there. You drop down into the shadow of an oak tree. Your heart is beating so loudly now you cannot hear if anything is coming. You look around wildly for a hiding place but there is none. You start to run. Blindly, without care, you race forward as fast as you can. Brambles catch at your clothes and roots and branches seem to curl around you, but you rush on.

You can hear laughter and the thud of hooves on the forest floor. You run on and on as a herd of red deer springs from the undergrowth and leaps over, around and past you in an instant. At their front is a milk-white hind, her eyes wild and her breathing ragged. She disappears between the trees. The hoof beats grow louder and a stag thunders out of the bushes. His hooves hit the ground like lightning bolts, his antlers crack against the trees and his breath roars around you like a hurricane.

Then he is gone and the forest is still once more. You stand shakily and look around. No one is there, but you can hear faint laughter and the sound of reed pipes on the wind. You climb through the brambles to the edge of a clearing surrounded by a ring of hawthorns. The trees are hung with ribbons and rags and the branches are heavy with blossom.

Golden light fills this space. At the centre you see the Lady. She is clothed in flowers and she sits on the skin of a white hind. In front of her kneels the Lord of the Greenwood, dressed in green, the antlers of the stag at his brow. She is laughing as she takes him into her embrace.

You leave them together and start to walk back to the edge of the forest and the singing children.

Beltane Projects

Every witch, whether male or female, should wear a floral or leafy crown for their Beltane celebrations. Don't feel self-conscious about making or wearing a crown. There is something truly magical and transformative about seeing yourself decked in flowers and leaves for the first time. Suddenly you see an older self, a self who is more instinctive and more in touch with the seasons.

If you've never made a crown before, leave yourself at least an hour to do it. It is not a difficult job, but it can be fairly time-consuming. If you just want to make a simple chaplet then twining ivy around your head is all you need to do. The ivy

will twist together so you won't need to use wire or string. For a more elaborate crown of flowers or oak leaves you need to complete a two-part process. The process is the same for both crowns.

FLORAL OR OAK LEAF CROWN

• First make your base of ivy. If you are a male witch you may prefer to choose twining honeysuckle as a base, because this plant is known to follow the course of the sun during the day.
• Select the flowers or oak leaves you want to include in your crown.
Goddess crowns: If you are actually making your crown on the eve of Beltane, and can find hawthorn in blossom, choose white may flowers for your crown. If, as is more likely, you are making your crown a day in advance, choose white flowers if possible, or just go wild with any blossom you have to hand.
God Crowns: If there is no oak in leaf, you can use other trees associated with the God, such as ash or blackthorn.
• De-thorn the stems and then tie the blossom or oak leaves in small posies, or bunches, using a tie that will degrade naturally such as green gardening twine or aluminium wire.
• Starting at a point that you have decided is the front, tie your best blossoms or leaves in place.
• Work backward, covering the stems and string of previous bunches with the blossom or leaves of the next bunch.
• In this way you will produce a ring of flowers or oak leaves with no stems or ugly string on show.

BELTANE APHRODISIAC LOVING CUP

No Beltane celebrations would be complete without the loving cup. This is a large bowl, or chalice, filled with alcohol, fruit and flowers which is passed from male to female with a flirtatious kiss.

Here are two recipes, one traditional and one modern. If you prefer not to drink alcohol you can substitute fruit juice or fizzy water.

TRADITIONAL BELTANE LOVING CUP

• Fill a bowl with chilled May wine. This is white wine in which a good handful of sweet woodruff sprigs have been soaking for 24 hours. If you can't find fresh, dried woodruff works just as well.
• Add the same quantity of chilled champagne and a small measure of elderflower cordial.
• Stir and serve.

MODERN BELTANE LOVING CUP

• Fill a bowl with a layer of crushed ice.
• Cover this with a layer of icing sugar and another layer of sliced strawberries. Pour a wineglass of brandy over the sugar and strawberries.
• Carefully top up the bowl with chilled champagne and float fresh flowers on the surface.
• Borage, cottage pinks, roses, clover, violets and pansies are all both beautiful and edible.
• Pass the bowl from male to female with a kiss.

Above
After their rites, many witches leave their crowns in the woods as offerings of thanks to the Goddess.

Left
Effervescent, alcoholic and refreshing, the Beltane cup is passed from priest to priestess with a kiss.

Midsummer Solstice

Solstice derives from the Latin sol (the sun) and sistere (to stand) and means 'sun stands still'.

Magical Correspondences

Element: *Fire*

Magical tool: *Wand*

Compass point: *South*

Season: *High summer*

Time: *Midday*

Age of mankind:
Prime of life

Attribute:
Action / energy

Gods and Goddesses
Bona Dea, Erce, Freya, Dana, Baal, Llew, Apollo, Helios, Dagda, Oak / Holly King

The midsummer solstice heralds the longest day and the shortest night of the year. It is the midpoint in the annual journey of the sun, the moment when the solar disc stops briefly at its zenith before continuing the cycle with its slow descent toward winter.

In Wicca, midsummer is seen as a celebration of the God at his most virile and potent. The solstice is a period of rest and respite, of abundance, peace and power. This would certainly have been true in older cultures when midsummer marked a blissful interlude between the rigours of planting in spring and harvest in autumn.

While Wiccans celebrate the strength of the God and their expectations of the coming year, they also acknowledge the solstice as a point of no return. After the solstice the God slowly begins to lose his power until his death and the later birth of a new God at Yule.

In some Wiccan traditions, the Holly King gains ascendancy over his twin the Oak King at midsummer. At the height of the sun's power, dark triumphs over light, introducing the theme of 'death in life', which will be played out fully at Lammas.

Many current folk customs across Europe still mark the strength of the sun and its descent by the lighting of huge fire wheels. These wheels are traditionally rolled downhill toward rivers or lakes. The symbolism of the fire wheel plunging into water echoes the death of the sun as it sinks into the western ocean. It also highlights the ability of water to reflect and, in doing so, to contain the fertile, healing power of fire.

FIRE AND WATER

Many solstice traditions involve both the lighting of bonfires and ritual bathing, usually in the early morning dew. Flocks were driven through the flames and, as at Beltane, the ritual fires were believed to drive out disease. At the same time, the potency of the first powerful rays of the solstice dawn were thought to be trapped within the morning dew. Many folk customs involved washing in dew, gathering dew on sheets and saving bottles of dew to be used in healing.

It was considered essential at one time to drive your stock down to a holy well or spring so that they could drink water that had been infused with the early sun. To fail to do so would be to invite illness and barrenness among the flock. Irish Celts would also mix the ashes of the solstice bonfire with dew and sprinkle the mixture around their homes to protect them from harm.

As with most pagan celebrations, the summer solstice was annexed by the early Christian Church. While condemning pagan rites, the Church was unable to stop them. Instead, a saint's day was attached to the solstice in an attempt to alter its significance. The Church was very careful in its choice of saint and declared 24 June to be the commemoration of St John the Baptist. It was hoped that while celebrating the solstice, pagans might include St John in their rites and that he would eventually oust the sun God as the focus of the ritual.

St John is depicted as a 'wild man of the woods' in the Bible. He is said to dress in animal skins and to feed on locusts and honey, food and clothing provided by hunting and gathering rather than agriculture. In biblical accounts, Salome, who is responsible for St John's death, performs the ritual 'dance of seven veils'. Some scholars believe that this dance echoes that performed by the Goddess Inanna on her descent into the underworld.

Inanna allows her lover, the sacrificial king, to die so that she can return to the world of the living. It is interesting to note that, like the Oak King, St John dies at midsummer. St John's main task is ritual baptism, or bathing, which again ties him to traditional solstice activities.

SOLSTICE HERBS

The two herbs most often associated with the solstice were *artemisia vulgaris* (known as mugwort) and *hypericum perforatum* (St John's wort). Artemisia is sacred to the Goddess Artemis and was used in the treatment of ailments connected with childbirth. St John's wort was believed to be a powerful protective herb, which would drive away any evil. At their solstice revels, unmarried women would wear a garland of mugwort around their waists and heads while unmarried men wore garlands of St John's wort. These garlands were then tossed into the flames for protection in the coming year.

Below

Aligned to the rising of the midsummer sun, Stonehenge is a focal point for pagan worship in Britain.

The Sun in Splendour

PREPARATION

On the day of your rite, spend as much time in sunlight as you can. Take care not to get burned, but feel the heat of the sun on your skin and the warmth of the earth underfoot. Notice the brightness of the light at this time of year.

If you can find *artemisia vulgaris* (female witches) or St John's wort (male witches), make yourself a belt of leaves to wear at your rite. Gather some wild, purple heather to decorate your altar.

Spend some time meditating on the things that the God brings to your life and consider which of them you value most. You might want, for example, to think about themes such as energy, wisdom, courage, sacrifice, action and endurance. Of course these are in no way exclusively 'male' themes, but in this instance you may want to consider them as gifts of the God.

You will need eight orange or gold tapers or tall candles and a small bowl of water. Make sure the candles are in steady holders or, better still, fill a large bowl with sand and push the candles into the sand. You can then place the smaller bowl containing the water into the middle of the ring of candles.

Pour a little sunflower oil in your ritual bath and add a handful of nasturtium leaves and nettle tops (don't worry, they won't sting you). Swirl the leaves around in the hot water.

THE RITE

Open your circle in the normal way. Relax and allow your breathing to deepen and your mind to become still.

Begin the solstice meditation pathworking.

Open the circle in the usual way.

You may want to sing to invoke the Goddess into your circle. Any folk song of love and longing would be appropriate.

Or you might like to say instead:

*'Queen of the wood, Queen of the hive
You, who are as sweet as the
heather on the hill
Be with me on this night of beauty
Lend your power to this, my rite.'*

When you feel the energy of the Goddess enter the circle, invoke the God. You will probably feel that you want to welcome him with drumming and dancing. You could also say:

'Lord of Light, I know the strength of your power. The fields are filled with the coming crop. The woods are filled with the climbing vine. The earth is warmed by your light and everything grows and thrives. Be with me now.'

When you feel the energy of the God enter the circle, light your fire wheel. Light the tapers one at a time. As you light each candle, name a gift of the God which has helped you to grow over the past six months. When all the candles are lit, the water will be filled with the reflection of the flames. Say:

'As the wheel turns, so must all things change. Light to dark, life to death, youth to age. As the oceans contain and reflect the power of the sun at its height, so may this water hold and reflect the power of this wheel of flame. May it preserve the healing power of life and light throughout the coming darkness.'

Sprinkle some of the water over your heart and head.

Drink some wine and eat one of the cakes. Spend some time meditating on the gifts the God has given you.

Close your circle in the usual way.

Make a libation to the Gods.

Sit next to your sun wheel and wait in vigil for the solstice dawn to rise.

Left
Many pagans make their way to Stonehenge to celebrate the dawning of the sun at the summer solstice.

Oak & Holly

Become aware that you are standing on a high, open moor. The air is cool and the last stars are fading from the morning sky.

You have spent this brief night in vigil, waiting for the solstice dawn. As the sky brightens and the first pink rays of pre-dawn light begin to warm the land, you can see below you a flat plain stretching into the distance. This plain is planted with fruit and wheat and barley.

You turn and begin the climb to the top of the moor. As you brush against the banks of purple heather, clouds of pollen and the scent of honey fill the air. You reach the top of the hill to find yourself in a huge circle of standing stones. In the middle of these there is a stone altar facing toward the east.

You enter the circle and kneel in front of the altar, your eyes in line with the rising of the sun. You notice a small bowl-like depression in the centre of the stone and see that it has filled with dew.

The sun is just below the horizon now and sends out rays of gold and scarlet light. The sky is painted with peach and rose and copper as the sun rises ever higher. The first shaft of gold light reaches across the land. On the plain, the fields of brilliant green shoots shine gold. On the moors, the heather shimmers with drowsy bees, their wings gilded by the sun.

As the sun rises, the shadow of one of the stones stretches toward the altar. The shadow lengthens further and further, until its tip plunges into the pool of dew.

With the sun fully above the horizon line, you stand and raise your arms in welcome. The heat is intense. You see a tall figure before you. He is dressed in gold and his cloak is worked with wreathes of oak leaves and acorns. Honey-coloured flame spirals around his shining limbs and crackles through the crown of oak on his brow. He carries a great spear, from which crimson flares blaze and flicker.

You step back, blinded by the golden brightness, and the figure moves toward the altar. He places the tip of his spear in the dew in a gesture of blessing and the water immediately begins to boil and hiss. A golden mist rises from the boiling dew and falls around the altar to spread down over the moor toward the fields below.

The golden figure kneels and drinks from the bowl of dew. He bows his head low until it enters the shadow. For a second his light seems to dim and then he stands again, shining as before. He turns and walks away from you.

As he goes you notice the light around him has taken on a silvery cast. The oak and acorn pattern around his cloak seems to have been replaced with holly berries and dark holly leaves now sit at his brow.

You kneel again, fill a cup with the golden dew, raise it to the sun and drink. Then you make your way down across the moor toward the plain.

Midsummer Solstice Projects

SOLAR OIL

You can use the healing power of the solstice sun to create a protective solar oil. First you have to find a source of fresh Perforate St John's wort (*Hypericum perforatum*). While it is illegal to pick endangered wild flowers (see the resource section for details), you can pick St John's wort provided you only take a little from each location, leaving the plants plenty of time to recover. The flowers are five-petalled and brilliant yellow, with pin-like gold stamens. The leaves are mid-green and oval, set opposite each other on branching stems. A mature plant grows to about 1m/3ft in height. The real test is to hold a leaf up to the light. If it is *Hypericum perforatum*, you will see hundreds of tiny translucent perforations on each leaf.

This plant was once considered so effective in driving away evil that it was named *huper eikon*, which, in Greek, meant 'overcomes apparitions'. Such was the plant's reputation that sprigs of it were hung at every door to repel dangerous spirits. Those suffering from nervous complaints or mental illness took the plant as a relaxant. In recent times the power of St John's wort has once again

Right
St John's wort oil can be used in solar rites and to contact the healing power of the God.

come to attention and it is now used by many as an antidepressant. Magically, the plant is believed to ward off demons, thunder, lightning and the attention of unfriendly witches.

Approach the plant at midday and, if you feel you have been invited, gather a large handful of leaves. Do not take so many that you put the plant under stress. Thank the plant and leave it an offering of a little fertilizer.

Next take a clear glass jar and fill it with the leaves. It's best to use a small jar and pack it full to the top. Cover the leaves with organic sunflower oil and leave the sealed jar in the heat of the sun from 11 June to St John's Day, 24 June. Over time the oil will become an increasingly darker shade of red until it resembles blood. Strain off the oil and store it in a dark jar.

You can use the finished oil to soothe nerve pain such as sciatica or to speed the healing of wounds. St John's wort oil is a particularly effective remedy for cuts and burns (however, it may cause sensitivity to light in some people).

In rituals, the oil can be used as a libation to the sun king or used to consecrate wands.

MAKING A WAND

Before you begin, take time to consider what you want your wand to achieve. Will you use it to invoke a particular element, for healing work or for protection?

Consider the type of wood for your intended purpose (there is a table of magical trees in chapter 6, page 180). You also need to think about how you want your wand to look and feel. Some witches believe that all magical work should be carried out in moonlight and will only work at night. I think that, as wands are ruled by fire, it is fine to collect your wood during the middle of the day, when the sun is at its height.

I believe the best wood for wand-making would come from a branch that had snapped off the tree but was still suspended in its branches. I always prefer not to cut a tree unnecessarily. However, there are plenty of witches who feel equally strongly that we are entitled to take what we need from nature and have no compunction in taking a living limb.

If you do take a living branch, always ask permission of the tree and pay attention to the answer. If you feel you have been invited to, cut quickly and cleanly. Catch the branch as it falls so that its power is not 'earthed'. Do not leave a ragged, damaged stump as this will allow infection into the body of the tree. Always leave an offering, either of your vital bodily fluid, or of fertilizer.

You can either leave the bark on, or strip it, then sand and oil the wand to a smooth finish. Hollow out a space at one or both ends of the wand to hold your choice of crystal (see the resources section for crystal correspondences). You can 'glue' these in place using melted pine resin or gum arabic, but take great care as pine resin is inflammable. Bind the crystal firmly in place with cord or leather. You can then finish your wand with the appropriate runes, spirals or personal symbols.

Above
Ruled by the element of fire, a wand can be particularly effective in directing solar energy.

Below
No matter how simple, creating your own wand will make it your tool, dedicated to your magical work.

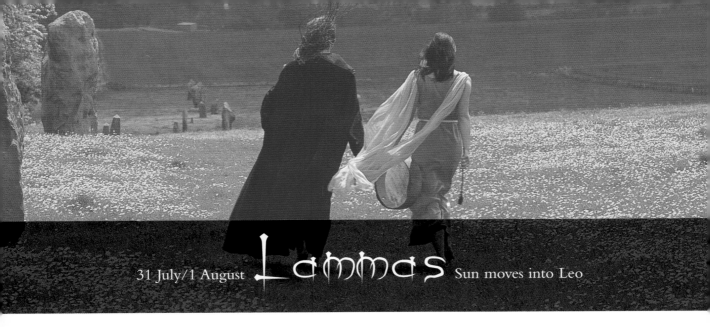

31 July/1 August **Lammas** Sun moves into Leo

Lammas falls at the beginning of the harvest, at a period of abundance and thanksgiving.

Right
A high priest and high priestess return from their Lammas rites.

Like most Wiccan festivals, it contains the seed of its opposite, an acknowledgement that all things pass. At the time of greatest bounty, when the first crops are being gathered and the earth is at her most fruitful, some Wiccans honour the 'death in life' aspect of the Goddess.

It is at this point that the God offers himself as a sacrifice and allows his blood to be spilled on the fields. His sacrifice, like that of countless vegetation deities before him, ensures the future fertility of the earth. The 'destroyer aspect' of the Goddess takes the God back into her embrace and he retreats under the soil to rule as the Lord of the Underworld. He no longer exerts influence over the mating of humans and animals, or the fertility of the land. Instead he becomes a model for those facing death and the wise consoler of the bereaved. In this role his gifts are knowledge, strength and acceptance.

THUNDER AND LIGHTNING

Lammas is also known as Lughnasadh, which means 'the mourning of Lugh'. Lugh was a Celtic deity of fertility and like many such his symbols were fire, in the form of the lightning flash, and water,

in the form of thunderous rainstorms. In early accounts his face was said to be as radiant as the sun. Lugh stood for everything the Celts valued in their culture. He was adept at every art and craft, a diplomat, a lover and a warrior. Lugh's worship may have extended all over Celtic Europe and many cities, including London, were named after him. London was known by the Celts as Lugh's fortress, Lugdunum, which later evolved into the Latin Londinium.

In the mythology surrounding Lugh, it appears that, symbolically, his main task was to preserve the knowledge associated with cultivating land. On one famous occasion, Lugh overcame his enemy Bres in battle but spared his life on condition that Bres shared his secret knowledge of agriculture. Lugh also overcame his grandfather Balor in battle. Balor represented the older and wilder forces of nature – powerful and fertile, but unconcerned with the prosperity of mankind. Balor's aim was to reclaim his land in battle, to transform farm into forest. In overcoming Balor, Lugh preserves the cultivation of the land and the harvest, ensuring the prosperity of the tribe.

In time Lugh's power failed and he was replaced in myth by his son Cu Chulain. Over the years the folk memory of Lugh faded, until he was known simply as 'Lugh cromain' (little hunched-over Lugh), a tiny, fairy craftsman dwelling under ground.

The name was corrupted and Anglicized to our present-day 'leprechaun'.

Every year, at the beginning of August, the ancient Celts celebrated Lughnasadh, and the date is still marked in Ireland today. The current Irish Gaelic for the month of August is Lunasa. There is some debate about whether Lugh originally held the festival to honour the death of his stepmother Tailtu (who died clearing a vast forest to make way for farming) or whether it was a wake in honour of Lugh himself. Whatever the origin, the holiday was a celebration to mark the start of the harvest and the sacrifice that went with it.

Most present-day Wiccans do not participate in the actual harvesting of grain, but they can and do participate in the symbolic meaning of the harvest in a very real way. Lammas marks the beginning of the culmination of a year's work, whether that work has been magical, spiritual or physical. It is the time when Wiccans acknowledge the sacrifice, whether of time or effort, that has to be made if any project is to come to real fruition. At Lammas, Wiccans celebrate the fruitfulness of the Goddess, while at the same time acknowledging the sacrifice of the God.

First Fruits

PREPARATION

Take a walk in the country and try to find the first blackberries of the season. In the garden check for early apples, pears and plums.

Pick a bunch of flowers, herbs or ripe stalks of grain, which symbolize the sun. Sunflowers are an obvious choice, as are calendula (pot marigolds), fennel, St John's wort and wheat.

Decorate your altar with early fruit and flowers, a sickle if you have one and red or orange candles.

Make a corn dolly.

Before your rite, spend some time thinking about the themes of sacrifice and productivity. Consider those things that you may have had to give up or leave behind over the last year in order to get where you are today. Consider how your own harvest is progressing. Are you happy with what you have achieved so far?

Place a handful of oatmeal in muslin and tie it into a bag. Place this in your ritual bath.

Most important of all, bake a loaf of bread for use in your rite. Treat the process as one of meditation. Involve yourself in the alchemy of bringing the yeast to life with warmth (hot water) and food (sugar). Concentrate on the magic of mixing masculine grain and feminine water. Watch as the two substances become a single living thing, growing and rising. Finally see the transformation that results in a finished loaf.

THE RITE

Cast your circle and open your quarters in the usual way.

Relax, allow your mind to become still and let your breathing become slow and regular. Begin the Lammas meditation pathworking.

Take a few moments to collect your thoughts, then continue with the ritual.

You may want to perform a circle dance to welcome the Goddess. You could say:

'Blessed Goddess, I welcome you on this night of birth and death. The harvest is begun, gardens and fields are filled with fruit and grain but we know there can be no life without death. We know that you are She who gives and She who takes. Be with me tonight.'

You may want to drum to invoke the God. You could say:

'Corn King, be with me tonight. You are the chosen one, he who will die to protect the land. Shining one, your time has passed. The harvest is begun, the fields are gold and the first fruits are ready for picking.'

Lift the loaf of bread from the altar and place it in front of you. Then take the flowers and grain, which symbolize the sun. Walk deosil (sunwise) around the bread and, as you walk, rub the grain and flowers so that the petals and seeds fall in a circle on the ground. Say:

'Corn King, go into the grain. You have lived and like all living things, you must die. Go into the grain, so that it is filled with the mystery of life. Corn King, go into the grain. So it was of old and so it is and so it will always be, as the circle spins forever.'

Lift the loaf from the earth and break it in half.

Drink some of the wine and eat some of the bread. Meditate on the ideas of sacrifice and fruition.

Close your circle in the usual way.

Make a libation to the Gods.

Left
During a Lammas ritual, falling grain symbolizes the fall of the God. Like the grain, he will rise again in the new year.

Below
The largest man-made sacred mound in Europe, Silbury Hill embodies the creative energy of the Goddess.

Spiral Dance

Become aware that you are in a garden. It is late evening, the sunk is sinking fast but the twilight still holds all the dry heat of the day.

The ground is dry and tiny clouds of white dust puff up around your feet as you walk. The air is heavy with the scent of ripe fruit. Strawberries and currants glow scarlet in the dusk and the subtle musk of raspberries rises round you through the hot air.

The garden lies beside vast acres of ripe wheat. You hear drumming and you step through the gate into the wheat-field and begin to follow the sound.

The beat of the drum is low and insistent, almost like the beat of a heart – a slow, steady, rhythmic pulse that carries through the evening air. As you walk, the ripe heads of wheat stroke softly against your thighs. The beat of the drum is the sound of your step and the song of the brushing wheat as you walk. You reach the top of a small rise as a sickle moon slides up over the horizon to hang low in the hot, night sky.

In the valley below, you can make out a group of women. They are wearing robes in all the colours of the early harvest – pale gold, silver and green – and their cloaks shimmer like ripe wheat as they turn and tread. Hands linked and held high above their heads, they are marking out a slow, stately dance. Step and turn, step and turn, step and turn.

You move closer and see for the first time a man among them, robed all in gold and standing to one side of the dancing women. The dance continues and the women stoop to lift up silver sickles, which gleam in the moonlight. The drumbeat is faster now and as they dance the women lean sideways to slice through the wheat. On they dance, through the field. They reap as they go, leaving a bare spiral behind them. The drumbeat is faster still and the dancing women spiral back toward their starting point.

They begin to leap through the air as they slash wildly at the ripe wheat. Their calls and wails sound loud through the night air. Faster and faster they whirl until they form a spinning circle of blades.

One of the women breaks away from her sisters. She plucks a sheaf of wheat from the ground and holds it above her head. The dancing stops and the women fall silent. The priestess raises the sheaf, raises her sickle and with one swift cut, she severs the ripe heads from the dry stalks. Behind her the robed man falls to his knees to lie among the stubble.

The women take off their cloaks, which are lined with crimson silk, and lay them over the body. In silence they leave the field. Below you, the light of the moon casts a pool of blood-red light over the fallen man. You turn and walk slowly back to the garden.

Lammas Projects

CORN DOLLY

The corn dolly or corn 'idol' is an ancient harvest symbol and one that is still found all over Britain. It was believed that the spirit of the corn would leap into the dolly as the grain was cut down. The harvest spirit could then be preserved safely in the dolly until the following year.

The Five-Straw Plait or 'neck' is the easiest to start with for a beginner. It grows into a spiral tube, which you can make as long as you like. The finished spiral can be tied in decorative loops or left to hang straight. You can cut the straw you need from a field or order it from a craft suppliers. Always soak the straw for about half an hour before use so that it becomes pliable and doesn't snap.

1 Tie five straws together below the ears.
2 Turn the whole thing upside down so the ears are now below the straws. Fan the straws into a flat star. You may want to number your straws with a pen at the start.
3 Fold straw 1 neatly and tightly over straws 2 and 3 (and leave it sticking out between 3 and 4).

4 Fold straw 3 over straws 1 and 4 (leave it sticking out between straws 4 and 5).
5 Fold straw 4 over straws 3 and 5 (leave it sticking out between 5 and 2).
6 Fold straw 5 over straws 4 and 2 (leave it sticking out between 2 and 1).
7 Fold straw 2 over straws 5 and 1 (leave it sticking out between 1 and 3) and so on.

Each time the straw being folded passes over two corners, it is left and the one at the last corner is picked up and used in its place until the round is completed. You can keep adding straws (just slide the fresh straw inside the last piece of the old straw) until your dolly is the required length.

MAKING RITUAL CANDLES

Ritual candles are really very simple to make. All you need is a quantity of beeswax, some wick cord and a mould.

• First oil the inside of your mould.
• Feed your wick through the mould and tie it to a pencil so that it is more or less taut and hangs in the centre of the mould.
• Plug the bottom of the mould with plasticine or modelling clay.
• Melt the candlewax. Take care not to overheat the wax as it is highly flammable. It is best to melt it in a bowl set over a pan of water. This will take some time as beeswax is very dense. If you want to speed up the melting process, you can grate the wax first.
• Carefully pour the wax into the mould and leave to set.

If you want to make candles for individual sabbats you can add fresh or dried herbs, flowers, fruit, seeds and berries to the wax before you pour it into the mould. You can also scent your candles with the appropriate essential oils. Always add essential oils just before you pour the wax into the mould.

Below
These simple round Sabbat cakes symbolize the full moon.

SABBAT CAKES

Most Wiccans use biscuits (cookies) for their 'cakes and wine' ceremonies. This, slightly adjusted, medieval recipe produces thin oatcakes.

15ml/1 tablespoon white bacon fat (or vegetarian lard, which, for some, is less gruesome)
110g/4oz/1 cup pinhead oatmeal (this must be true meal, not 'rolled oats' or 'porridge oats')
Large pinch salt
Large pinch of bicarbonate of soda (this is not in the original recipe and can be left out – but it helps)
A little tepid water

• Melt the fat and stir into the dry ingredients.
• Bind to a soft dough with the water.
• Sprinkle some oatmeal onto your board and gently knead the dough to remove the cracks.
• Roll the dough as thinly as you can.
• These oatcakes were originally cut into farls or triangles.
• For esbats, cut the oatcakes into a full-moon shape.
• For sabbats and special occasions, cut crescents as well as rounds and fix them together with a little water to form the symbol of the Triple Goddess)O(.
• Bake on a hot, ungreased 'girdle', or a heavy-based frying pan, until they begin to curl up at the edges.
• Remove with a palette knife and leave them to dry out under a very low grill (broiler). They should become crisp but not toasted brown.
• When cool, the oatcakes will stay fresh for over a week if sealed in an airtight container.
• For extra crispness, pour a layer of salt into your container, cover with a clean tea towel and place your cakes on top of the towel.
• You can add ingredients that are appropriate to each sabbat, such as honey at the summer solstice or poppy seeds at Lammas.

Above
Used in every Wiccan rite, candles represent the energy of the element of fire and can be decorated with strips of wax to suit each rite.

Below
A simple five-strand plait or 'neck' is the easiest corn dolly for a beginner.

Autumn Equinox

At the autumn equinox, day and night are of equal length for a short period, as they were in spring.

Magical Correspondences

Element: *Water*

Magical tool:
Chalice

Compass point:
West

Season:
Autumn

Time: *Evening*

Age of mankind:
Old age

Attribute: *Feeling*

Gods and Goddesses:
Morgan, Epona, Lilith, Dionysus, the Horned God, Bacchus.

Right
At the point of balance in the year, Wiccans reconnect to the land.

Where the earlier equinox was a time of conception, full of the potential for growth, this time of year is one of thanksgiving for that which has been successfully accomplished.

Wiccans honour the God, whose vital energy has gone into the soil to promote growth and also into the grain to preserve next year's harvest. This idea of the grain holding the dynamic force of the God was one of the great truths of ancient agricultural religions. In the Greek Eleusinian mysteries, initiates were taken through a symbolic death and rebirth and, as a final revelation, were shown a single head of wheat.

In early harvest rites it may well have been the case that the king offered himself as a sacrifice and his blood, or ashes, were spread on the fields to purify and protect them. There is currently discussion about whether human sacrifice actually took place in early pagan societies – if it did, it probably conferred a great honour on anyone who willingly offered his life for the good of the tribe.

It would probably have been unthinkable for early communities to continue for long without a king to represent and embody the vital force of the God. The rites would have been undertaken immediately after the symbolic death of the old God to ensure the continuation of the divine power in the newly appointed king.

Wiccans acknowledge both the fruitfulness of the Goddess and the energy of the God when celebrating the completion of their own individual harvests. This might be an actual harvest of fruit and vegetables, or a symbolic harvest of their magical or spiritual achievements. Wiccans also acknowledge that the autumn equinox is the point at which the Goddess withdraws her fruitful energy from the earth.

DEATH AND REBIRTH

Many Wiccans have adopted the story of Persephone in their equinox celebrations. Persephone was the daughter of the Goddess Demeter, and Demeter's role was to bring forth life. She was responsible for the fruitfulness of the land and its crops and flocks

In Greek myth, Hades, the God of the underworld, abducts Persephone and makes her his queen. When Demeter discovers her daughter has been taken, she starts to grieve and to search the earth for her. While she mourns she withdraws her fruitfulness from the land and the earth begins to die. Finally Hades is forced to allow Persephone out of the underworld

and back to the surface of the earth. He does so on condition that Persephone returns to him in the underworld for several months of the year. When her daughter is with her, Demeter is happy and the land flourishes. When Persephone is taken back below ground, Demeter grieves and the earth's fruitfulness ceases.

At the autumn equinox, the sun is about to enter the sign of Libra and many Wiccans take time, at this point of balance, to assess and to give thanks for what they have achieved. Like the grain, gathered in the harvest and stored for the following spring, each achievement can be seen as the seed of the coming year's activities.

Harvest Home

Preparations

Take time to walk in the countryside and to gather wild nuts, fruit and berries. Use some of this harvest to decorate your altar, but preserve what you can, either as jam, jelly, cordial or wine, so that you have a sense of the fruit of the harvest continuing through the seasons.

Decorate your altar with corn, grain, nuts and fruit. You will also need a ball of twine, a tealight and a pomegranate.

Before you start your rite, lay out a simple spiral of twine on the ground, so that you will walk sunwise (deosil) into the labyrinth and starwise (widdershins/ anticlockwise) out of it. Make the spiral as large as your ritual space will allow and try to ensure that you make three circuits of your spiral before you reach the centre. Place the pomegranate at the centre.

As you did at Lammas, bake a magical loaf, but this time mould it into the shape of a man. This will represent John Barleycorn, the spirit that goes into the grain and which we have cut down to create both our bread and our beer.

During your ritual bath, meditate on the idea of the essence of the sun's power being transformed into the grain, which both sustains us as food and forms the seed of next year's harvest. Think too about the themes of balance, the turning of the wheel and the idea of death and rebirth.

Above
A John Barleycorn figure made of bread is left in the woods as an offering.

Right
The spiral symbolizes both the Goddess and the turning point of the year.

The Rite

Open your circle in the usual way.

Relax, slow your breathing until it becomes deep and regular, and allow your mind to grow still.

Begin the autumn equinox meditation pathworking. Then raise the cone of power.

Invoke the energy of the Goddess into the circle. You could say:

'Demeter, mother of corn and grain, keeper of the mystery of life, be with me tonight. The earth has turned and summer is gone from us. Like you I grieve to see the plants dwindle and decay. Life must give way to death, youth to age and light to dark, but the womb of darkness brings forth the seed of light and after death comes rebirth.'

When you feel the energy of the Goddess enter the circle, invoke the God. You could say:

'Lord of the Underworld, whose spirit has gone into the earth and into the grain, be with me tonight. Comfort me as the darkness grows and life retreats from the land. In the midst of warmth and plenty, give me the courage to face the coming winter.'

When you feel the energy of the God enter the circle, take your lit tealight and slowly walk into the centre of the spiral. As you walk, meditate on the turn of the year and the growing darkness.

If you want to acknowledge that death comes to us all, then eat one of the pomegranate seeds. If not, then simply think about the seeds of new growth contained within the fruit.

When you are ready, blow out your tealight and make your way slowly out of the labyrinth.

Drink some of the beer and break up the body of the John Barleycorn loaf. As you are eating the bread, remember the mystery of the grain.

Close your circle in the usual way.

Offer your libation to the Gods.

The Grain

Become aware that you are standing on a high plateau. It is late afternoon and in the distance you can hear the crash of surf breaking against the shore.

The air is cool and as you start to walk, the sun begins to sink slowly toward a line of hills that mark the horizon. On both sides, the path is lined with brambles, their arching stems weighed down with glossy blackberries. Bees hum through the last remaining flowers. Behind the hedges the harvest is gathered in and lies in glowing stacks in the fields. The stubble glitters like gold thread in the evening light and through the stalks you can see patches of warm red earth.

You walk on across the plain, passing orchards of apples, plums and pears. Windfalls rot beneath the trees and drunken wasps drone from fruit to fruit through the long grass. A mist begins to rise around you and the smell of a distant bonfire prickles your nose. Pale wisp-like tendrils of fog curl around your feet as you walk.

The path curves sharply to the left and cuts across a small waterway. As you cross over the stream you come upon a woman sitting on the bank. She is wearing a black cloak and she is veiled in white. At her feet is a large cauldron filled with water. In this she washes a sickle with great care. The water runs first red, then black, then clear. She motions you to sit by her, then points to the surface of the water.

As you look into the cauldron, a thread of mist appears to drift across the surface.

It clouds the water and then fades, leaving a clear view of the scene unfolding before you. You see the figure of a hooded woman. She is dressed in white and gold and carries a pomegranate wand. She stands grieving on one side of a river. On the other side of the fast-flowing water are two more figures. One is a young woman dressed in green and next to her, holding her by the arm, is a man. His skin appears to be dark, almost blue, and he is dressed in a black cloak.

As you watch, the young woman reaches out across the water in a gesture of farewell. Then she and the man turn toward the entrance of a cave. At the cave mouth a white candle and a black candle are burning brightly in shallow alcoves. The couple enter the cave and are lost from your view.

The woman in white falls to her knees and covers her face with her hands. As she weeps you see the plants around her wither and die. The leaves on the trees decay, fruit begins to moulder, the crops in the fields rot to nothing and a terrible silence falls on the land.

The water suddenly stirs and boils and you look up again. The woman points to a basket at her side. She lifts a cloth to reveal a single ear of wheat. 'This is the mystery,' she whispers. You look again at the wheat and when you lift your eyes, you find the woman gone.

Autumn Equinox Projects

Above
Many Wiccans bake their own loaves and decorate them with spirals and pentacles for their rites.

Right
Cleanse your chalice in fast-flowing water before you consecrate it.

John Barleycorn Bread

There is something truly atavistic about tearing to pieces and eating the body of the sacrificed corn king. To make John Barleycorn, you will need:

700g/1½lbs/6 cups of plain flour. You can also use wholemeal flour, or mix in a handful of oatmeal, dried fruit, nuts or rye flour, provided you end up with the correct amount of ingredients.

50g/2oz butter

Level teaspoon salt

Scant ³⁄₄ pint hot water

1 pkt dried yeast (or scant 25g/1oz fresh yeast activated in some of the hot water with a teaspoon of honey)

• Warm the flour, either in the oven or in a microwave (for about 45 seconds).
• Add the salt and yeast (if dried).
• Melt the butter in the hot water and add to the dry ingredients (if using fresh yeast, add to the remaining hot water).
• Knead for at least 10 minutes until you have a springy, elastic dough.
• Model your dough into shape. You can use God images like the Cerne Abbas Giant as a template. The main thing to keep in mind is that the figure should be very male – you can make this bread as rudely priapic as possible, given the constraints of working in dough!
• Leave the dough to rise for an hour in a warm place.
• Glaze with egg (and poppy seeds if you like) and bake for 40 mins at 190°C, 375°F or Gas mark 5.

Choosing a chalice

Autumn is ruled by the element of water, so it's a perfect time to look for your chalice. If you simply want a chalice to contain the wine on your altar, you can choose any type of goblet you like. Glass chalices come in a variety of colours and decorative finishes. Blue or green glass reinforces the symbolism of the element, while clear glass will allow you to see the blood-red wine or golden mead within.

If you want to use your chalice outdoors or for potion-making, you should consider something a bit sturdier. Chalices can be found made of pottery, wood and metal. Pottery is probably the best choice – wooden chalices are beautiful but if you fill them regularly with liquid they tend to crack. Metal chalices are heavy to carry and can taint the contents. Pottery is also fairly weighty but, if glazed, makes the best container for both potions and wine.

If you are creative, join a pottery class and make your own chalice, which will bear exactly the right words or symbols.

Magical Cords

Most Wiccans wear cords, whether they are working 'skyclad' or robed. These can symbolize an individual witch's degree or, when tied in a loop around the waist, can symbolize the circle of the cosmos. Cords can also be used for knot magic. As it is tricky to make cord, most Wiccans buy them from haberdashers. However, you can plait together strands of unspun wool, which you can dye an appropriate colour.

In knot magic, nine knots are customarily tied in the cord, starting at either end and finishing with the final knot in the middle. The purpose of the spell is reaffirmed as each knot is tied and the final knot is closed with intent.

'By knotted one, the spell's begun
By knotted two, it cometh true
By knotted three, so mote it be,
By knotted four, the open door
By knotted five, the spell's alive,
By knotted six, the spell I fix,
By knotted seven, the stars of heaven,
By knotted eight the stroke of fate,
By knotted nine the thing is mine!'

Samhain

Magical Correspondences

Element: *Earth/Fire*
Magical tool: *Pentacle*
Compass point:
North west
Season:
Beginning of winter
Time: *Time outside time*
Age of mankind:
Decrepitude
Attribute: *Divination*
Gods and Goddesses:
Cailleach Bheur, Hag or Crone, Hecate, the Carlin, Lilith (Hebrew), the Morrigan, Kronos/Cronus, Pluto, Hades, Anubis

At Samhain, both the God and the Goddess have become Underworld deities and are dwelling below ground – the God in his role of keeper of the gates of death and the Goddess as the guardian of the mysteries.

The wheel of the year has turned almost full circle. Through the seasons, Wiccans have celebrated the birth of the new God and honoured his growth to power and inevitable sacrifice to protect the land. We have also seen the Goddess return, rejuvenated, to reclaim her place in the world as the Virgin. We have witnessed her transformation to Mother and finally to the wise Hag, ruling in the darkness.

Unlike the other Wiccan sabbats, which are firmly rooted in the seasonal cycle, Samhain feels as if it exists outside time. It falls at a point when the old year is dying but the new sun has yet to be born at Yule. Like its opposite, Beltane, Samhain is seen as a 'hinge' on which the year turns and, like Beltane, Samhain has always been considered a time when contact with the 'other worlds' is most likely.

At both of these great turning points, the world of magic and the world of ordinary life collide. To the Celts Samhain signalled the end of summer and the beginning of the dark half of the year. In Wicca, Samhain is the time when witches believe that the veil separating the worlds is at its most transparent. It is at Samhain that Wiccans honour and remember their dead. Many witches use this 'time outside time' to undertake divination or to try to commune with their ancestors. They do not actively try to summon or call back the dead in the same manner as spiritualists holding seances, but rather make the ancestors welcome, should they care to come.

FEASTING AND SACRIFICE

Just as Beltane saw early communities herding their flocks to upland pastures, so Samhain marked the return of flocks to their winter pens. The final harvest would have been fully gathered and communities would have had to slaughter any cattle or sheep that they could not feed through the winter. Samhain would surely have been a time both of great feasting and of sacrifice to the Gods. As at Beltane, purifying fires were lit across the country, but this time it was the bones of the butchered animals that were burned. So great was the slaughter at Samhain that November later became known as the 'blood month'.

Samhain would also have marked the onset of a time of great fear for early communities. Winter, when food stocks were low and people were surviving on what they could hunt, was the most dangerous season of all. Individual deaths would have been common, along with doubts about whether the tribe would survive until the spring.

As at Beltane, household fires were doused and a central bonfire was lit. In Ireland, Druid priests lit the central purifying fire, from which all other flames across the country were taken. Accounts also describe this great bonfire as a place of execution and human sacrifice. Wiccans treat Samhain as a time to remember their dead and to contemplate their own mortality, to 'feast with death'.

Samhain is perhaps the most widely recognized of the pagan festivals, celebrated by pagan and Christian alike as the holiday of Halloween. In Mexico the period is a joyful celebration known as Los Dias de las Muertos, 'the Days of the Dead'; in Catholic countries the festival of All Saints and All Souls is a solemn remembrance of the deceased.

Typical Halloween activities, such as wearing fancy dress, 'trick or treating' and carving pumpkin lanterns are likely remnants of early pagan rites. Priests or shamans may well have blacked their faces with soot and dressed in skins or costumes in order to commune with the spirits of the dead. Early communities certainly made offerings to the dead and to the fairies, which they believed would expect gifts on that night. This later evolved into the tradition of 'guising', which entailed gangs of youths visiting each household in turn to beg for food, money or firewood for the bonfire. With the emigration of many Irish and Scots to America, the tradition evolved again into its present incarnation – 'trick or treating'. The custom of lighting torches and lanterns is probably the oldest of all. Flaming torches would have provided strong sympathetic magic for those trying to drive away unwelcome fairies or spirits. The addition of frightening carved faces would have made the lanterns all the more effective.

Above
The power of the Crone is the power of the wise woman. She is a source of knowledge, mystery and, ultimately, regeneration.

The End of Summer

PREPARATION

It can be quite difficult finding a quiet time to perform your ritual on the night of 31 October as groups of children will inevitably be banging on your door in the hope of getting treats. It obviously makes sense to wait until children are in bed before beginning your rite. Stewart Farrar makes the sensible suggestion of having two celebrations in *Eight Sabbats for Witches*. He advises holding a secular costume party on the night of Halloween to which you can invite non-Wiccan guests and take part in 'trick or treating', and then having a proper Wiccan rite later on.

Decorate your home and your altar with symbols of the dead. You could take Mexican *offrendas de las muertos* altars as inspiration. These are decorated with skulls and with paper skeletons and coffins. Use black candles on your altar in honour of the dead. Place a set of runes, tarot cards, a pendulum or a black mirror next to your altar.

Carve a pumpkin lantern for your altar.

Spend some time meditating on the themes of death and rebirth. Consider the necessity of rest and regeneration before birth and growth.

In your ritual bath pour a few drops of cypress, patchouli and rosemary essential oil. Cypress is traditionally associated with death and rebirth, patchouli is known as 'graveyard dust' in many ancient spells, and rosemary is the herb of remembrance.

THE RITE

Open your circle in the usual way.

Relax, allow your breathing to become slow and regular, and let your mind still.

Begin your Samhain meditation pathworking. Take a few moments to collect your thoughts, then continue with the rite. Invoke the God and Goddess into the circle. On this night it would be quite appropriate to welcome both the Goddess

and the God with slow, rhythmic drumming like that of a heartbeat.

When you feel the presence of the Gods in your circle, welcome them by saying something like:

'Lord of death and resurrection, keeper of the gates of underworld, I welcome you to this circle, this time outside time. Lady of mysteries, here, between the worlds, I honour you. Lend your power to my Samhain rite.'

Now is the most auspicious time to undertake divination. If you have tarot cards or have made a set of runes you could use these. If you have neither cards nor runes, you can simply look into the candle flame or into your bowl of water.

You may also want to contact the ancestors. A good way of clearing the mind in preparation is to chant the vowel call. This is made up of the five vowels AEIOU that are found in many languages. Slowly chant 'Aah, Eh, Ee, Oh, Ooh' three times and then wait to see if any of your ancestors make contact.

Finally blow out the altar candles and quarter lights one by one. Before blowing out the final light, say 'I feast with death'. In darkness drink some of the wine and eat one of the cakes.

In silence relight the altar candles. Thank the Gods and then leave the circle. It is traditional on the night of your Samhain rite to leave the quarters unclosed and to leave a special offering of food and wine for the spirits.

DIVINATION

Samhain is considered the best time for divination because it falls at a great turning point of the year: the boundary between the worlds is more diffuse and access to other realms is easier. Try scrying or watch the flames on your altar. You may be surprised with what you discover.

Feast with Death

Become aware that it is night. You can smell smoke in the air and you look up toward the ocean of stars overhead.

Behind you a long barrow cuts starkly across the night sky, black against indigo and diamond. Along the ridge you see beacon fires flaring against the darkness.

The silence is suddenly filled with whoops, yells and screams as a band of cavorting dancers leaps from behind the barrow. Their faces are covered in soot and lengths of dry straw hang down from their hats like hanks of white hair. They are carrying torches, rattles and drums, which they shake and beat frenziedly. They whirl around you for a second and are gone.

You reel backward, almost falling, but a cold, hard hand catches your arm and pulls you close. You cannot really see her in the darkness, but you know this ancient creature is as old as time. The coldness of her thin fingers on your flesh is the coldness of death. You try to shake her off, but her grip is tight. She leans forward, her face blue in the icy night air, and places a bony finger to her lips. She squats down behind a tumble of fallen rocks, pulling you down next to her. You try to prise off her fingers, but she is immovable. She says nothing, simply points with her chin to the sky. When you see what is coming you drop down in the shadow of the barrow.

The noise of the dancers was nothing compared to the tumult of the screaming gale that sears across the plain. It beats you flat against the ground, whips your hair around your face and steals your breath. The night is filled with the sound of howling. Above the wind, you hear the thunder of hooves beating louder and louder. From where you lie you can see the screaming, fluttering, swooping madness of the Wild Hunt as it careers across the sky. You turn your face to the dirt.

The horde is gone. You lift your head to see the last ragged wing disappear and you lie back exhausted against the side of the barrow. You notice the crone is gone, before you fall into a strange, waking slumber. You feel yourself sinking slowly back through the side of the barrow and into the hollow heart of the mound.

You are surprised to find lights here, flickering below the ground, and many cavernous rooms. All around you, caves and tunnels reach down in every direction. You follow a tunnel on the left. It curves down deeper and deeper and you feel yourself moving into the heart of the earth. A dark figure stands at the entrance to one of the caverns. He carries a spear in his right hand. You edge past him and stare at the walls. They are covered with the imprint of a hundred hands, chalk white, soot black and ochre, red as blood. In the gloom Aurochs leap and bellow above you, wild horses buck and prance, deer strut across the plain. On one side of the wall a great female figure is carved from the stone. She leans forward in childbirth, straining breast, belly and thigh. Opposite her a male figure rises up in his power, crowned with the antlers of a stag.

The hooded figure in the doorway looks down at you. He puts out the glittering lights, one by one. As he carefully pinches out the last flame, he whispers 'Feast with death'. You lie down, at peace, among the bones of the ancestors.

In time you wake to find yourself lying once more against the flanks of the barrow. You can hear quiet laughter and the scuffling of feet, far away below the mound. Dawn is finally breaking and you rise slowly and turn for home.

Samhain Projects

MAGICAL OAK GALL INK

This recipe comes from Graham King, who runs the Museum of Witchcraft in Boscastle, North Cornwall. It creates indelible black ink, which, unlike modern ink, grows darker with age. The ink is ideal for use in the creation of magical amulets, for recording spells or for scrying. Oak gall ink was used in medieval manuscripts and has lasted so well that these texts are still easily legible, several hundred years later.

To make oak gall ink, you will need:
A handful of oak galls. These are found on the stems of almost every oak tree. They look like brown wooden marbles and are created by the larvae of a wasp. Only take galls with tiny holes in them, which means the larva has left the gall.
   Half a pint of water
   Some very rusty nails (or, if you want to be a purist, iron ore)

• Grate the oak galls as finely as possible – a nutmeg grater is ideal for this job.
• Put the galls, water and iron in an old pan and boil gently for 15 to 30 minutes.

• If you can heat the ink outside, do, because it does not smell at all pleasant while boiling.
• Cool, strain through a coffee filter paper and store in a dark jar. You may find mould grows on top of the ink. Simply strain again and rebottle. This ink lasts indefinitely and continues to darken in the bottle.

THE DARK MIRROR

The easiest way to try scrying is simply to pour some oak-gall ink into a dark glazed bowl. The ink creates a perfectly black reflective surface.

   If you want to make a dark mirror from glass, you will need:
   A circle, or oval, of glass. If you go to a glazier, they will cut and bevel the edges for you so that the glass is safe to handle.
   A circle, or oval, of wood, several inches wider than the glass. Make sure you carefully sand down the wood so that it is smooth to the touch.
   A can of black spray paint (this is one of the few times when modern technology really helps).
   Epoxy resin/hot glue gun.

• Place the glass on the wooden base and draw round it.
• Outdoors, spray the back of the glass with two coats of black paint, allowing to dry between coats. Do not be tempted to touch it until it is completely dry.
• Place a thick layer of epoxy resin or hot glue all over the inside of the circle you drew on the wood.
• Very carefully position the glass and drop it into place on the glue, paint side down. This is the trickiest part. It is not easy to realign the glass if you put it in place slightly askew. The glue will take the black paint off the back of the glass. So take care and when the glass is in place don't touch it until the glue is dry.

Below

Oak-gall ink can be used for spells and talismans and also for scrying. Here it creates a reflective, black surface.

• You will now have a black mirror and can decorate the surround as you wish.

SLOE GIN

Sloes are ripe from September onward, but are better picked after the first frost. They are found on blackthorn bushes (*Prunus spinosa*), which have white, hawthorn-like flowers and lots of spines. By October, the fruits are blue/black with a grape-like bloom. Although they look like tiny plums, don't be tempted to try eating these fruits – they taste awful and make your mouth pucker up.

They do, however, give a wonderful aromatic flavour to gin. Sadly it is impossible to re-create this drink without using alcohol, so if you are a teetotaller you will miss out.

To make sloe gin, you will need:
Bottle of gin
500g–1kg / 1–2lbs sloes
Sugar to taste (approximately 150g / 6oz / 1 cup)

• Prick the sloes and place them, with the sugar and gin, into a 'Kilner jar' (or any large sealable jar).
• Leave them for about four weeks, agitating the bottle every day.
• Strain into a clean bottle, label and store in a dark cupboard.
• Sloe gin lasts almost indefinitely. You can drink it at Samhain in honour of the dead, or at your Yule celebrations.

Above
Surrounded by the last withered blooms of solar honeysuckle, this sloe gin is infused with power of the old year. Used in ritual, it gives access to the great mystery of death and rebirth.

Left
When scrying, witches often angle the surface of their black mirrors to reflect an altar candle. They then interpret the flickering dance of the flame.

The Course of the Moon

Wiccans celebrate every full moon by casting a magic circle. Esbats are usually less ruled by the seasons and are instead devoted to honouring the Gods and to the making of magic. Obviously the period of the full moon is considered highly auspicious for casting spells or developing psychic and intuitive skills, and it is at this time that magic is believed to be at its most effective.

PREPARATION

Before your rite, reflect on what you hope to achieve. This might be a specific piece of magic or a desire to learn more about a particular Goddess or God. Once you have decided what you are aiming for, plan out either the spell or the invocation that you believe will be most effective. If you are new to writing spells or chants, allow yourself plenty of time. Nothing is less conducive to creative thinking than a feeling of being rushed.

If you find the process difficult (and many witches do when they first come to try writing things down), be creative. Allow your mind to roam. Jot down anything that you feel is connected with the subject, make lists of correspondences, places, colours and feelings, make a note of anything you believe usefully sums up the subject about which you are thinking. You might want to do a bit of research into mythology, or even read some poetry, just to get your mind working.

When you have a mass of material, collect your ideas and begin to put them on paper in an order that has meaning for you. Eventually you will have your invocation or spell fully worked up and ready to use.

Right

Taking time to bathe in moonlight will help to attune you to the changing energies of the moon in her various phases.

ESBAT RITE

Open your circle in the usual way. Relax, allow your mind to still and your breathing to grow deep and regular.

Begin the esbat pathworking. Then Allow yourself a few moments to collect your thoughts and then invoke the Goddess into the circle. You could call her by one of her many names – Diana, Artemis, Callisto, Hecate, Arianrhod or Selene – or you could call her with a chant you have written yourself.

When you feel the Goddess enter your circle, invoke the God. You could say something like:

> *'Lord of the dark wood and of the moonlit glade, come to me now.*
> *Lord of hoof and of horn, come to me now*
> *Lord of corn and grain, be with me now and lend your power to my rite.'*

You could also welcome the God with your own chant.

Next perform your spell, incantation or pathworking. Drink some wine and eat one of the cakes.

Close the circle in the usual way. Finally, offer your libation to the Gods.

MOONRAKING

In England, country witches have long used moonraking to make magic at the full moon. First they make a moon rake, which is a six-foot (two-metre) pole with a carthorse shoe attached to one end. Next they assemble the equipment needed for the spell: a large basin, an earthenware jug of water (some use their own urine) and a mirror. The mirror is placed in the basin, covered with water or urine and floated onto a still pond. Then, the moon rake is used to position the basin so that the moon's reflection is caught in the mirror. Once the power of the moon has infused the liquid, the basin is 'raked' out of the pond and the fluid poured into the jug, to be used in the spell the witch has planned. Later, the liquid is boiled and poured into running water to deactivate it.

Moon Mysteries

Become aware that it is dark. The night is still and clear. The air is filled with the scents of the sea, fecund, salty and abundant. A bank of soft, white sand stretches ahead of you.

At your feet is a tangle of driftwood and seaweed; the tide line is picked out with foam and glittering shells. You are standing on the strand looking out to sea. As you watch, the moon begins to rise over the ocean. First you see a crescent of cream-coloured light. It is crisp, opalescent and perfect. Then, slowly, the primrose-yellow orb of the full moon sails up over the horizon, weightless and buoyant.

A beam of pale light falls across the waves, creating a shining path from the shore to the distant horizon. The huge silver globe floats, luminous, against the violet sky.

You are bathed in warm silver light. The waves gently ebb and flow at your feet. You feel each ebbing wave pulling you closer to the ocean. Carefully you step into the foaming froth of bubbles on the shoreline and, to your surprise, the path of silver light holds you up.

You find that you are moving forward and upward without having to walk. You feel the gentle breeze blowing softly against your skin. You raise your arms as if in flight and feel the silvered air lift you and carry you forward.

As you are carried closer to the face of the moon you begin to see a figure, whose size defies understanding. She is holding the moon in her arms as if it were a child. She is visible but invisible. Her body seems defined simply by the movement of the great constellations of stars. Still, you can see her and the suggestion of a pearl-white robe falling from one shoulder. Her skin is unseen and yet appears to be a pale alabaster. Her hair falls in luminous ivory streams, which are, at the same time, nebulous and indistinct.

She speaks and you do not hear, but you understand everything in the deep centre of your heart. Every fibre of your being thrills to the call of that soundless voice. The ebb and flow of the tides of space surround you and you find yourself rocked in the cradle of the universe as the moon is rocked in the arms of the Goddess.

You have no sense of the passing of time. Time and place have no meaning here. The turn of the season, the turn of a lifetime are all one. This place is changeless and eternal.

After a period, which may have lasted seconds or aeons, you begin to descend through the cloudless sky to the waters below. You feel the effervescence of the salt spray against your legs and you step out of the waves onto the shore.

The moon is high overhead now and you spend the rest of the night watching the progress of its ivory globe as it sails across the velvet blackness of the sky.

Chapter 4
WORKING ALONE

Working as a solitary witch means that you are responsible for your own magical and spiritual development. Of course the same is ultimately true of everyone, but in a coven the new initiate is surrounded by people who have years of experience and who are happy to help and advise them as they move forward. One of the major roles of the High Priestess and High Priest is to monitor their initiates' progress and to guide them toward the specific practice or knowledge that will help them to grow as witches. Without a coven to advise you, you will have to manage your own studies.

Be methodical, consider each individual area of your magical life and then decide how you can improve on it. The most obvious task to set yourself is to read.

Read as much as you can on mythology, on local folklore and traditions, on other religious paths and, of course, read about witchcraft and its history. Use your powers of discrimination – books that offer 'genuine 100%-effective love spells' or 'hexes for every occasion' may not be the best source of information. Go back to basics, read Gardner, Doreen Valiente or Sybil Leek and again, be discriminating. Don't accept everything you read as 'gospel' – make your own judgements.

Keep honing your skills. Consolidate on what you have learned and then expand on what you can do. Polish your ability to visualize until you are really proficient. Continue to practise handling and moving energy until it becomes second nature to you. Learn your invocations off by heart.

Make time for ongoing learning. Don't forget that one of the meanings of wicca is 'wise one', so decide what you want to learn about and pursue it wholeheartedly. You may choose divination or herbs and healing. Either of these fields will offer a lifetime of interest and discovery. An interest in the tarot, for example, may lead you to a study of symbolism, the Qabalah or even the history of the playing card and its use in fortune telling. Studying herbs will broaden your knowledge of the natural world and could introduce you to medical herbalism or homeopathy.

Remember to assess your own progress. You will have to be scrupulously honest with yourself – set regular goals, then make a note of whether you achieve them. This process fits naturally into the cycle of the seasons, with seed ideas being sown in spring and achievements harvested in autumn. Your goals should be a mix of practical tasks, such as learning how to make a wand or robe, intuitive skills such as divination and finally, personal spiritual development. Only you will know if you are actually forming meaningful relationships with the natural world, the elements and the Gods.

Finally, step back occasionally and look at yourself from the outside. It can be very easy when you are new to the craft to get completely caught up in it. Make sure that you devote as much time to your work, family and friends as you do to Wicca.

Be aware also of how you may appear to others. Many people who have just discovered Wicca feel they ought to look the part and start sporting a large, shiny pentagram and what they imagine to be 'witchy' clothes. Think about why you might want to broadcast your new identity in this way and consider the limitations of a 'uniform' – you might conclude that it is far more magical to be able to slip through a crowd unnoticed than to stand out. Invisibility allows freedom.

Left
Working alone means you are free to approach your Gods however you wish, through chanting, drumming or ecstatic dance.

Personal Evolution

It has been pointed out many times that, in the 21st century, there is little need for a religion based on the fertility of people or crops. Over-population has reached crisis point and, in the west, 'agribusiness' with its heavy use of chemical fertilizers has caused such a glut in production that farmers are now paid not to plant crops. So why are people still drawn to Wicca in a world that is dominated by industry and the Internet?

The whole point of following Wicca as a path is that it helps us to evolve as individuals, both emotionally and spiritually. Through ritual, through knowledge of the magical elements and the forces of nature, we can discover how to come into contact with the Gods. It is the mystical truth that results from communion with the Gods, which is the ultimate aim of Wicca. Like many other religious paths, Wicca offers an inner experience that is greater than the 'real' or outside world. Self-knowledge is a by-product of seeking this inner experience. If we are prepared to change in line with such knowledge we will find our lives empowered.

MYSTERY AND RITUAL

You may have been drawn to Wicca originally by a desire to cast spells, to make magic, or to brew potions. If, however, you hope to approach the true mystery at the heart of Wicca, you have to be willing to devote time to meditation and ritual and, above all, you must be prepared to change.

Within Wiccan rituals, whatever their form, there is an essential truth that touches us profoundly. While outwardly dealing with fertility and the cycle of crop production, Wiccan ritual is a means to help practitioners experience mystery. The repetition of ritual, of incantation and invocation, reaffirms a pathway and allows us access to this inner mystery.

Robert Cochrane once described witchcraft as 'bringing man into contact with God and man into contact with Self'. He also suggested that it is through a growing understanding of the mystery involved in communing with the divine that we come to know ourselves and begin to attain wisdom.

A DIFFERENT WORLD

If you continue to meditate, to undertake ritual and to pursue communion with the Gods, you will discover that, in time, your attitudes change and you see the world differently. You will find it less easy to apportion blame to others or to the world for what happens in your life. Instead you will discover how to take responsibility for your actions. You will find that, in situations where you may once have lost your temper, you no longer 'rise to the bait'.

You will come to accept responsibility for creating balance in your life. This is never easy as it usually means having to put an end to repeating fixed cycles of behaviour. If, before you became a witch, you were always in the wrong relationship or the wrong job, you will now have to address the problem and try to solve it. Behaving in new ways takes us outside our 'comfort zone' but it can be both exhilarating and liberating.

Finally, with practice, you will be able to judge when you really need to use magic to achieve your ends or whether it is best to leave things as they are. Before making important decisions you will find yourself taking time to consider seriously the outcome. Weighing up your actions and their consequences is one of the great responsibilities – and rewards – of living magically.

Right
Resourceful, strong and self-aware, all witches know that they are responsible for their own lives.

Self-dedication

You have spent the last 'year and a day' observing the changing rhythms and tides and attuning yourself to the seasons. You have developed your skills in visualization and handling energy and have decided that you want to work as a solitary witch. Whether you continue to work alone or decide to seek out a coven later on, it is useful to formalize your present devotion to the craft in a self-dedication ritual. This will give you a sense of true commitment and will make your intent clear both to your higher self and to the Gods.

In fact, you can only be 'officially' initiated into a traditional Wiccan coven by a Wiccan high priestess or priest. However, there is no reason why you should not make a meaningful and serious dedication of yourself to the worship of the Gods, to the honouring and protection of life and to your personal growth. It is only after the rite that you will discover whether you have indeed stirred your deep mind and 'initiated' a new aspect of yourself. If you allow yourself to be guided by the Gods you may find that you have indeed begun a process of rebirth into a new magical existence.

Of course, anyone undertaking a self-dedication ritual will not be entitled to join others in traditional Wiccan circles. They will not be qualified to initiate anyone else into a Wiccan coven, nor will they have access to the Book of Shadows, to the rituals, or to the magical techniques of an established Wiccan coven. The ritual will only have a personal meaning for the individual involved. However, if you decide to work alone, a ritual that is significant for you is all that matters. If you later find a coven that you wish to join and which accepts you, they will initiate you into Wiccan traditions.

THE MAGICAL QUEST

When you are certain, beyond a shadow of a doubt, that you want to make a commitment to the Craft of the Wise, you need to choose a significant date for your ritual. It might be one of the sabbats or the next full moon. Whatever date you choose, make sure you give yourself at least a month to prepare.

You should already have made, or found, all the tools needed for your rite, during the last year and a day. In the month leading up to your rite, sleep with your athame under your pillow and record all your dreams during this period. Don't be surprised if you dream of travelling, or of moving house. These are typical dreams for those on the brink of making a major life change. Set aside time to spend with the elements. During your month of preparation, find the time to get into the countryside regularly.

If at all possible climb a hill, or mountain, to get in touch with air – at the very least try flying a kite. Use your magical map and spend time in the eastern quarter at your favourite meditation spot. During your air meditation, the element may make itself known to you in some way. A feather might fall from the sky, or a breeze might blow a leaf or a dandelion seed into your hair, or across your path. Take this for the sign it is and collect your elemental gift with thanks.

To encounter fire, you could sunbathe (provided your ritual is to take place in summer) or light a barbecue or bonfire. If you don't have a garden then lighting candles will do. Again you could go to your existing fire meditation spot. Be mindful of your surroundings. You may find something you are prompted to offer as a gift in the ashes of your fire. You might spot a particularly vivid red flower or some hot chillies in a local market on one of your walks. Any of these would be acceptable elemental gifts for fire.

To encounter water, go swimming, book a flotation tank session or visit the sea. Spend plenty of time showering or bathing to bring yourself into contact with the element. On the seashore, there will be no shortage of shells or interesting bits of seaweed begging to come home with you. At a lake or stream you might simply want to collect a little bottle of the water as a gift.

Finally, to encounter earth spend time in the countryside. Braver souls might want to try potholing or caving. If you can't get out of the city you can still usefully spend your underground (subway/metro) journeys meditating on earth. Once again, be observant. Keep your senses open to any rock, seed or plant that may offer itself up as a gift.

A MAGICAL NAME

Most witches choose (or are given) a new magical name when they are initiated. As you plan to dedicate yourself to magic you too should choose a new name that reflects your magical aspirations. Give it a lot of thought. Every time you say your name in a magic circle, you will be reaffirming your magical aspirations to the universe. Be wary of choosing something very grand, or the name of a God or Goddess – don't fall into the trap of seeking the wrong sort of power. Instead look for inspiration in the world of nature, plants and animals or even mythology, and keep your name secret. If you hear your private name in a dream or vision, you will know the Gods are contacting you.

Above

A priestess returns to the cave where she undertook a spirit quest to find her magical name.

At One with the Elements

A meditation – in which you undertake an elemental journey, encountering each of the elements – prepares you for the coming ritual.

This meditation is designed for the solo practitioner. You may prefer to record it onto a cassette (it takes 10–20 minutes), then play it back during your rite.

THE JOURNEY

Become aware that you are standing on the edge of an ancient forest. The night is calm and still. A pale, full moon sails slowly across the velvet sky. It casts a clear silver light and you can see easily. You begin to walk into the heart of the wood.

You are wrapped in a thick, woollen cape the colour of the earth beneath your feet, a subtle weave of brown and green and grey. On the woollen background, intricate patterns are worked. Fox, badger and hare are entwined with wolf, bear and stag. Otters dart, salmon leap up and owls swoop through the design. Twisting around the hem of the cloak is the figure of a huge serpent, which coils around an egg, to grasp its own tail in its mouth.

You walk on through the cold night air, glad of the warm cloak. All around you are the sounds of the forest and the creatures of the night. Bats flit above your head, while underfoot mice and voles skitter through the grasses. The ground begins to drop away and you follow the path downward into a clearing. At the centre is the mouth of a cave. You enter the dark. Here the light of the moon fails and you make your way forward by touch alone. The cave turns into a tunnel, which spirals down to the right. Using all your senses you creep forward, your left hand

on the outer wall, spiralling into the darkness. You make your way deeper and deeper down, into the centre of the earth. The roof above you is penetrated by roots, which reach down to stroke your face gently. The air is warmer here and sweet with the scent of the soil and the soft, dry dust beneath your feet.

You walk deeper into the dark, until the tunnel widens into a huge underground cavern. You lie down on the cave floor and listen to the silence of the earth.

You are at peace, here in the womb of the earth, deep in the fertile darkness. Your limbs relax completely, there is no tension in your body, only rest and peace. You hear nothing and in the deep silence your past begins to slip away from you. Here, there is only sweet silence and darkness and the warm earth beneath your body. Your thoughts begin to drift. You are forgetting your earlier life. All is quiet, all is calm, here within the body of the Great Mother.

Time passes. The blink of an eye or the passing of aeons is all one to you now, in the depths of the earth. All you can hear is the beat of the earth's heart, steady, regular and slow. You are at peace. You lie in silence.

Far, far away you hear a murmur, the softest sound, as of a ripple gently running across the surface of a still pool. A liquid whisper, that seems to swell against the earth walls and roll toward you. The sound continues to flow toward you, eddying into the crevices in the rock and rolling ever nearer. This is the sound of water, flowing underground toward the sea.

In the darkness the soft sound of the water grows louder. As you lie still you hear the gentle lapping of waves against the rock walls of the cavern. You are at peace, listening to the undulating water as it rises toward you. You feel its soft touch, as the river begins to swell beneath you. Soft ripples stroke your skin.

You feel the earth sinking away as your weight is borne up by the water and you feel yourself lifted. You are drifting now, drifting in the darkness – drifting in the dark waters. You are completely at peace, floating in the inky darkness, floating on the limpid waters of the womb. You feel the current twirl you slowly out of the cavern and into the river. You have no direction – you are simply floating.

The river flows faster now and you are carried easily through the current. You hear the rising crash of surf up ahead. The tunnel seems to become tighter – the water rushes forward and, suddenly, you are outside under the vault of the sky, floating on the gentle swell of the ocean.

You lie back, letting the water carry you. Your cloak slips from your shoulders and swirls down into the depths of the ocean. Your memories sink with it, all the concerns of your earlier life, everything sinks into the deep and you float away. You are washed clean by the waves. Your mind is still – you are drifting in the limitless waters.

As you float you begin to feel lighter and lighter. Each breath you take seems to fill you more completely. You are at rest, floating in the waters of the deep. As each surge of the sea lifts you up, you feel lighter and still lighter until, with one final swell, your body rises up out of the ocean and floats into the air.

You are as light as air now, lifted like pollen on the breeze. You are weightless, formless, rising on the thermal tides. You glide upward. You feel lighter and lighter. You body is becoming shapeless,

you are a movement of air, a billow, a breath blowing across the universe. You rise higher and higher, feeling lighter and lighter. Your breath mingles with the air around you as you float like a bubble into the blue dome of the sky. Higher and still higher you float, weightless as the breath of the wind.

As you rise higher, the sky becomes darker and darker. Blue slips from indigo to black. You float on and the blackness is replaced by gold, vermilion and white as you drift into the fiery disc of the sun.

You feel no pain, only blissful heat as you float into the sphere of fire. Intense heat and limitless flame are all around you. Fire crackles along your limbs for a second before you become a creature of nothing but flame. You are filled with the radiant peace of fire. You are filled with power as the flame of life blazes through you. You are transformed by the flame. This is the crucible of change and you feel yourself altered forever by the fire. Your old life is burned away, there is no pain, only heat and energy and the rapture of change.

Suddenly there is nothing but silence and peace. You have forgotten the past as you float among the stars. You are quite still in the silence of the universe. You have no body, only being, and you are filled with the silence of the Gods. Here, in this divine silence, your earlier life is gone from you. Your plans, worries and achievements – all are forgotten in the velvet darkness. You are completely at peace – completely at rest. Your breath is the breath of the winds of the universe, your body is formless, immense, universal; your being merges with the divine silence.

A new existence is yours, a new beginning, a new life.

Rest in the arms of the Great Mother.

Now find yourself returning to your room and to your ritual. Feel yourself at one with the universe but back in your body and ready to continue.

Dedication to the Gods

THE DEDICATION

Before you begin your dedication ritual, ask for guidance from the Gods – they will answer. Think very carefully about what you are undertaking. In the future you may have to make real sacrifices for your faith. Decide what your aims are in following the Craft of the Wise, whether it be a deeper understanding of your self, greater knowledge of the natural world, a commitment to preserving the earth, union with the divine or a combination of all of these. When you are completely clear about your future magical aims, write these down as a dedication on a piece of paper.

PREPARING FOR THE RITE

Having chosen your name, collected your tools, undertaken your 'year and a day' of magical work and spent a month renewing your relationship with the elements, you may feel you are now truly ready to make your commitment to Wicca. Think carefully about the step you are about to make. If you still have to consult notes to cast a circle, if you can't visualize, or you feel that you have not mastered the basic handling of energy, you are not ready. Wait until you have acquired the right skills before continuing.

Try to spend the day on which you plan to undertake your rite walking in the country. Be alone with nature and listen for the voice of the Gods on the wind. If you want to be traditional, fast on the day of your rite; if you're not used to fasting have a snack and drink plenty of water.

Decorate your altar in the way you think will be most fitting and lay out all of your tools in position. Give thought to the meaning each tool has for you. Take special care in choosing the leaves and flowers that will decorate your altar.

Place your dedication oath and the gifts for each element on the altar.

As you did at Lammas, bake a 'magical' loaf of bread. If you have any home-made wine or beer use that, or choose something special, such as champagne, for your chalice.

Place a pair of scissors and a pin on your altar. Don't forget to set up a tape or CD player inside the circle.

Make up a special dedication incense and a blend of oils or herbs for your ritual bath.

During your bath, allow yourself to feel cleansed emotionally as well as physically. Wash away your past life and step out of the water as a new soul awaiting rebirth.

THE RITE

After your ritual bath, dress in your robe.

Open your circle in the usual way.

Relax, open your energy points and begin the elemental pathworking.

Allow yourself a few minutes to become aware of your body once more. Then stand and remove your robe. Spend some time acknowledging your physical body and what it really looks and feels like without its usual covering.

Take a gift to each of the elements in turn. Meditate in front of each quarter light. You may be offered a gift in return.

Dance, drum, sing and chant to welcome the Gods and say whatever you feel is most appropriate to welcome them to your circle.

Next, read aloud your dedication.

When you have done so, cut a few strands of your hair and place them on the censer. While they are burning, prick your finger with the pin and allow a drop or two of your blood to fall into the candle flame and into the bowl of salt water on your altar. Your blood is symbolic of your union with the Goddess and the God.

You will probably feel quite disconnected at this stage. Lie down again

Right

Removing your robe and working skyclad brings self-acceptance and an acknowledgement of your own body.

and allow your breathing to become regular. You could find that, as you lie in this trance-like state, the Gods may speak to you.

When you are ready, eat some of the bread and drink some of the wine.

Close your circle in the usual way. Offer a libation to the Gods. Spend some time resting and recovering from your dedication ritual. Those who have made such a dedication to the Gods often feel extremely emotional. You may feel euphoric, you may find yourself grieving for your earlier life.

Whatever the emotions, accept them and allow yourself time to regain your balance before returning to the everyday world of work, family and friends.

167

Chapter 5
THE PATH
CONTINUES

If you have undertaken the self-dedication ritual and spent some months, or even years, working alone, you may feel the time is right to explore working with others. There are now lots of ways of seeking out other witches. As a starting point, you could look through magazines – such as *Pagan Dawn, Hecate's Loom, Grail Directory, Green Egg* – and also contact the Pagan Federation, attend some open rituals or even visit pub moots (informal pagan gatherings).

By now your critical faculties should be fairly well honed. Be careful when meeting new 'witches', as not everyone who claims to be a witch really is one. There are some misguided souls who hide behind Wicca in order to gain power over others. Be extremely wary of anyone who claims that having sex with them is part of a first degree initiation. Trust your instincts and simply don't do anything that makes you feel uncomfortable.

There are now various study groups, which exist to introduce people to the basics of Wicca (there are details in the resources section). These groups are particularly useful because they provide an opportunity to take part in group rituals, to meet others who are interested in Wicca and, most importantly, to meet coven leaders. Certain coven leaders may be prepared to accept you into a training group that could lead to initiation.

Don't feel that the first training group or coven you encounter is necessarily the right one for you. It is true that some people are led to a coven magically and you can usually tell when this is the case

because everything slots together with extraordinary ease and a great feeling of homecoming. Most people however, have to go through a process of searching in order to find the right coven.

The best thing you can do is to assess how you feel in the company of the High Priestess/Priest. Are you comfortable? Do they inspire you with confidence, or do they seem muddled, vague and unsure? Is the High Priest/Priestess a victim of his or her own ego? Some people run covens for all the wrong reasons. They may be seeking to make themselves feel important, or worse, may need to feed on the emotional life of their initiates.

Finally and, possibly most importantly, do they have a sense of humour? If you join a coven you will be spending a lot of time together. Wicca is, of course, about devotion to the Gods, but it is also about *joie de vivre*. Could you imagine taking on several years in the company of someone who doesn't make you laugh?

Far left
Witches from various covens often work together, pooling their skills and energy to create powerful magic.

Left
Even those who are members of a coven regularly choose to spend time working alone.

Working In a Coven

Much of Wiccan ritual was inherited from freemasonry, and with it came the degree system. Traditional Gardnerian and Alexandrian Wicca has a system of three degrees, or levels, of initiation and these correspond to the level of commitment one is prepared to make to the craft.

THE DEGREE SYSTEM

Initiates are divided into first, second and third degree witches. The use of the degree system differs slightly from tradition to tradition, but is essentially the same. The first degree is for those who are new to the craft and it confers entry into a coven and access to all the experience and information to be found there and brings a connection to the coven group mind. The second degree is for those who want to devote their lives to the craft. They will be familiar with all aspects of running a coven and creating ritual and will be working on deep levels of personal development. The third degree is for those who have achieved inner balance and a unification of mind and body, anima and animus and true union with the Gods.

Some covens train first degree initiates from scratch. Others will insist on a 'year and a day' of training before initiation, giving would-be Wiccans the opportunity to learn, to undertake ritual and to explore their relationship with the Gods before making a commitment to the craft. It also gives them time for second thoughts. It is better to realize you have made a mistake before, rather than after, initiation.

During the first degree, the initiate will learn how to control energy and how to undertake any role in the circle, from casting to invoking the Gods, or having the Gods invoked onto them. They will

Left

Witches chant and dance to
raise the cone of power.

study and become proficient in at least one form of divination and will probably also be able to undertake basic healing, whether through touch, herbal remedies or spells. First degree witches will also either make or find all the ritual tools they need. During their training they will become accomplished at creating invocations, charges and rituals for esbats and sabbats.

One of the most important tasks of the first degree is to begin a personal Book of Shadows. This will be a record of all magical work undertaken and its efficacy, of magical insights, incense or wine recipes that were particularly successful, herbal remedies or dreams that were significant – everything that will become a personal store of magical wisdom.

DIFFERING TRADITIONS

In Gardnerian Wicca, attaining the second degree brings a new level of autonomy. The second degree witch has the power to initiate others into the craft to first and second degree and can 'hive off' and set up their own coven. Traditionally a priest initiates women and a priestess initiates men. In Alexandrian covens the second degree entitles you to play a full role in helping to run the coven, to create rituals and to help to train first-degree initiates. In both traditions, the second degree means a deep and life-long commitment to the craft and an ongoing pledge to serve the Wiccan faith to the best of your ability.

The third degree in Alexandrian covens enables the witch to undertake the same roles as the Gardnerian second degree, to initiate and to form a new coven. For Gardnerian witches, the third degree is the final coming together of the physical and the spiritual and signifies a deeper union with the Gods. In both traditions, the third degree brings with it the title of elder in the craft and acknowledges a deeper level of wisdom and knowledge.

Training and development

All covens undertake some kind of training and development. These are informal get-togethers, which may take the form of teaching discussions, magical pathworkings or practical workshops. These gatherings are a good way for the coven to get to know one another 'off duty', as well as to exchange ideas.

Essential training covers basics, such as what is expected of the initiate and how to behave when in a circle. Coven leaders require their initiates to be self-motivated and enthusiastic. Nobody is spoon-fed information in Wicca, everyone has to want the knowledge and to ask for it.

Circle etiquette teaches witches how to enter, move around and leave a circle. It shows them how to be aware, physically, of their fellow coven members, so that

people don't trip over one another in a rite or get in the way of the sharp end of an athame. Circle etiquette also explains the mechanics of ritual so that if someone has, for some reason, forgotten their role, somebody else can step in and open a quarter, or pass the appropriate tool, enabling the rite to continue flawlessly.

Most covens would include topics such as how to maintain concentration during visualizations or magical work. They would also encourage attention to detail, certainly in terms of any magic undertaken. Coven leaders would make it very clear that anyone working magic should be specific about what they want to achieve, careful about how they undertake magic to achieve it, and scrupulous about ensuring that any work done does not harm another.

Coven leaders will also expect their initiates to be aware of their energy and enthusiasm outside the circle. If someone always arrives without a bottle of wine, or never volunteers to set up the temple or help wash up afterward, it does not go unnoticed. Even boring tasks ought to be approached with care and commitment. After all, it is the energy that coven members put in, not just magically but in all areas, that keeps a coven dynamic and alive. If one person just cruises without any effort, everyone else has to work that much harder to keep things going. Development covers the acquisition of new skills that will widen a new witch's experience of the craft. It will certainly cover areas such as how to invoke effectively and how to handle the

experience of being invoked on. Initiates will be taught how to produce effective and meaningful rituals and how to manage the energy of these rites so that it is not dissipated or lost.

During their first degree training and development ('T and D') days, initiates may be offered workshops in drumming, dance, chanting, mask-making, potion-making, blending incense, creating talismans and voice work.

Creativity is at the heart of Wiccan ritual and development sessions will aim to stimulate the initiate's ability to create powerful invocations and charges for specific elements, Gods and Goddesses. Other creative gifts such as painting, carving, cooking and craft work are also encouraged, to be added to a growing repertoire of skills.

Training and development is aimed at creating witches who are competent at ritual work, able to express themselves creatively and open to new experiences.

Left, above and below During training, every member of the coven learns how to invoke the deities. Here the Goddess is welcomed and adored with the 'five-fold' kiss.

Assessing the 'Pros and Cons'

When you're trying to decide whether or not to seek out a coven in the hope of becoming a member, keep in mind that there are 'pros and cons' involved in every decision.

You already know the benefits of working alone – spontaneity, intimacy with your Gods, freedom of expression and the luxury of being completely selfish about what you do and when you do it. These are all things over which you have to compromise, to some extent, within a coven system. Most witches enjoy working alone and continue to do so in tandem with their coven work, a system that gives them the best of both worlds.

When they first join a coven, some people can find it very frustrating, for example, to have to arrange the dates of their rites to accommodate everyone else. In practice this often means that sabbats do not take place exactly on the traditional date, but on the nearest available Saturday. In fact, it is not necessary to follow the traditional calendar slavishly – Imbolc should take place when the first snowdrops are actually peeping out of the ground, Lammas is the celebration of the first fruits, not 1 August, and witches, of all people, should be tuned in to the seasons rather than an artificial calendar.

RESOLVING CONFLICT

Within every group, no matter how well the members get along, there is going to be friction at some point. Witches are only human and both egos and immaturity sometimes get in the way. Arguments may take the form of conflict over the aims of the coven, or silly squabbles over who does the most tidying up in the temple.

Sadly some arguments are inevitable, but most covens, like most families, have proven and effective ways of dealing with disharmony. If the high priestess and priest know their jobs, then these difficulties will be dealt with to the satisfaction of all concerned and balance will be restored. Being a member of a coven means having to be flexible and having to develop good social skills.

Of all the problems that might beset a new coven member, the most serious would be a clash with his or her high priestess or priest. If someone has been working as a solitary for some time it can be very difficult to accept instruction, or even criticism. A coven is not a democracy, however, and you have to accept that when you join. Ultimately, the high priest and priestess make the final decisions about how you progress as a witch within their coven. If you can't accept authority you really should reconsider the idea of joining a coven.

UNDERSTANDING YOURSELF

If you want to experience working with others, however, then the benefits of working in a coven far outweigh the problems. Being initiated into a coven is a testing process that teaches you a lot about yourself. As a new Wiccan you are accepted into a family of more experienced witches, all of whom are able and happy to share their knowledge with you.

Although covens don't exist to operate as therapy groups, if you are anxious or confused there will always be someone on hand who has had the same worry, or experienced the same difficulty, and who can give you support and guidance. Within larger covens there are numerous people willing to share their skills, whether it be to teach you how to read runes or make a tincture to cure a sore throat.

Covens that work well also generate a lot of magical energy. They will have established rituals and techniques that they know to be effective and, when you join a coven, you will have immediate access to these practices.

Finally, there is nothing to compare with the feeling of camaraderie and fellowship generated by a successful coven. This is partly because of the establishment of a group mind, which comes about during regular magical work. If all the members of a coven have the same aims and try to achieve them together, they become closer and closer. While they may not necessarily live in one another's pockets, coven members care deeply about each other and are always willing to help their brothers and sisters in the craft. Together they form a close-knit and dynamic magical team working with commitment toward a joint aim.

Whatever your final decision, whether to work alone or try to join a coven, you will find that Wicca offers you a path of spiritual growth and individual development. Working alone will bring you into an intense personal relationship with the divine and with nature, while working in a coven brings a new kind of magical energy and the closest bonds of friendship and care. Wicca is never an easy path, but it is one that brings untold gifts of joy and enlightenment.

Below
The high priest and high priestess running a coven together will aim to establish an environment of harmony and openness.

Chapter 6
RESOURCES

Working as a solo practitioner means that you don't have such easy access to the pool of magical skills and traditional lore found within a coven. You can't turn to your High Priestess or High Priest, or to a coven elder, and ask for advice on the best ingredients for an incense, the best day to undertake a ritual, or the most appropriate form of magic for a particular situation: instead you have to rely on yourself.

To help you begin making magic on your own, the following pages contain basic material on a variety of areas. There is an introduction to herbal healing and the magic of trees, a brief precis of the Celtic tree Calendar, and information on working with crystals, making incense and on various magical correspondences.

When you come to put together a ritual or a spell, you can refer to these tables and those on each element (pages 46–53) to find the most auspicious day and time for your magical work. Don't ignore this process when you are starting out. It is much better to plan everything thoroughly before you begin.

In the contacts section there are lists of useful addresses, should you want to find out more about study groups, pagan organizations or working in a coven. There are also lots of suppliers of high-quality, good-value magical equipment.

Most of these businesses are run by dedicated pagans and all of the organizations are run by pagan volunteers. If you get in touch, please always enclose either a stamped, self-addressed envelope or international reply coupons so that the people you contact don't have to pay to send information back to you. You can find reply coupons at your local post office and these can be exchanged for stamps in any other country.

Left
Skrying with a crystal ball enables the priestess to enter a deep meditative state.

TABLE OF ELEMENTAL CORRESPONDENCES

Elements	**Air**	**Fire**	**Water**	**Earth**
Planets	Mercury	Sun	Moon	Earth
Tarot suits	Swords	Batons	Cups	Coins
Tarot cards	Judgement	Strength	Temperance	The World
Magical tools	Athame	Wand	Chalice	Pentacle
Magical power	Divination	Evocation	Equilibrium	Geomancy/ Plant contacts
Runes	Dagaz	Inguz	Laguz	Othila
Directions	East	South	West	North
Seasons	Spring	Summer	Autumn	Winter
Moon phases	Waxing Moon	Full Moon	Waning Moon	New Moon
Times of Day	Dawn	Noon	Twilight	Midnight
Colours	Sky blue	Vermillion	Aquamarine	Amber
Perfumes	Mint	Basil	Rose	Patchouli
Trees	Aspen	Pine	Willow	Hawthorn
Precious stones	Topaz	Fire Opal	Emerald	Quartz
Astrological signs	Libra	Aries	Cancer	Capricorn
	Aquarius	Leo	Scorpio	Taurus
	Gemini	Sagittarius	Pisces	Virgo
Egyptian deities	Ma'at	Ra	Tum	Osiris
Greek deities	Hermes	Prometheus	Poseidon	Gaia/Demeter
Roman deities	Mercury	Vulcan	Neptune	Ceres
Parts of the body	Lungs	Circulation	Heart	Intestines/Skeleton
Jungian functions	Thinking	Intuition	Feeling	Sensation
Creation gods	Sky Father	Lightning Bolt	Great Ocean	Earth Mother
Elemental spirits	Sylphs	Salamanders	Undines	Gnomes
Archangels	Raphael	Michael	Gabriel	Auriel
Four watchers of the sky	Winged Angel	Lion	Eagle	Bull
Kabbalistic worlds	Yetzirah	Atziluth	Briah	Assiah
Tetragrammaton	Yod	He	Vau	He
Magical actions	To Know	To Will	To Dare	To Keep Silent

MAGICAL PROPERTIES OF PLANTS

PLANT	PLANET RULER	ELEMENT	GODS	MAGICAL USE
Angelica *A. Archangelica*	Sun	Fire	Solar Gods	Solar invocations. Cleansing and consecrating space, wands and candles
Apple *Malus sylvestris*	Venus	Water	Venus Bran, Olwen	Initiation (fruit of the Underworld), Lammas and Samhain rites
Bistort *Polygonum bistorta* **Warning: the berries are poisonous, only use the root**	Saturn	Earth	Pythia Serpent deities	Use the snake-like root in ritual baths to contact serpent energy
Blackberry *Rubus fruticosus*	Venus	Water	Triple Goddess fruits are first green, then red, then black (maiden, mother, crone)	Incense to contact the fey, leaves and berries infused or made into wine for use in rites. Leaves produce black dye for robes

PLANT	PLANET RULER	ELEMENT	GODS	MAGICAL USE
Calendula *Calendula officinalis*	Sun	Fire	Sun Gods	Incense and infusions for solar rites, anointing and protective oil
Dill *Anethum Graveolens*	Mercury	Air	Mercury, Hermes, Thoth	Clears the mind, raises the spirits. Incense oil, and infusions used to stimulate the mind
Hemlock *Conium maculatum* **Warning: Deadly poisonous**	Saturn	Water	Hecate	Deadly poisonous but can be laid on altar during invocations to Hecate or Samhain rituals
Lady's Mantle *Alchemilla mollis*	Venus	Water	Goddesses of Childbirth	In incense, particularly in hermetic magic/alchemy and to gain knowledge of the Goddess
Lavender *Lavandula officinalis*	Mercury	Air	Air and Underworld Deities	In incense, oils, infusions and ritual baths, lavender soothes and restores balance
Nettle *Urtica dioica*	Mars	Fire	Lightning Deities	One of the most useful magical plants. Use in incense, infusions oils, teas, beer, wine, as cloth and paper for spells. Nettle brings knowledge of the fertilizing power of the God
Patchouli *Pogostemon patchouli*	Venus	Earth	Venus Deities of Eroticism	Essential oil can be used in incense, oils and baths in aphrodisiac magic or to contact the element of earth
Poppy *Papaver somniferum*	Moon	Water	Underworld Deities	Poppy seeds can be added to cakes, bread, incense, oil and ritual baths to contact the underworld
Sage *Salvia officinalis*	Jupiter	Air	Father/Sky Gods	Use in incense, baths, oils and infusions for purification, consecration and wisdom

CELTIC TREE CALENDAR AND BETH LUIS NION (MAGICAL ALPHABET)

Tree	Month	Letter	Magical Properties
Birch	24 Dec–20 Jan	B (Beth)	Purification, creativity, birth, new ideas, projects
Rowan	21 Jan–17 Feb	L (Luis)	Protection, power, divination
Ash	18 Feb–17 Mar	N (Nion)	Power, rebirth
Alder	18 Mar–14 Apr	F (Fearn)	Journeying, oracles, support
Willow	15 Apr–12 May	S (Saille)	Witchcraft, moon magic, poetic inspiration
Hawthorn	13 May–9 Jun	H (Uath)	Purification, witchcraft, both purity and eroticism
Oak	10 Jun–7 Jul	D (Duir)	Gateways, protection, energy of the lightning flash, contact with the God
Holly	8 Jul–4 Aug	T (Tinne)	Energy of thunder, life essence, protection from poison
Hazel	5 Aug–1 Sept	C (Coll)	Wisdom, divination, dowsing
Vine	2 Sept–29 Sept	M (Muin)	Spiral of life and death, truth, overcoming inhibitions
Ivy	30 Sept–27 Oct	G (Gort)	Resurrection, change of consciousness, contact with the Goddess
Reed	28 Oct–24 Nov	NG (Ngetel)	Contacting the fey, energy of the sun king, established strength
Elder	25 Nov–22 Dec	R (Ruis)	Protection, the energy of fire, contact with the crone
Silver Fir	23 Dec–24 Dec, the day between the worlds	A (Ailm)	Birth, purification
Furze		O (Onn)	Energies of the spring equinox
Heather		U (Ura)	Energies of the summer solstice, passion
White Poplar		E (Eadah)	Energies of the autumn equinox
Yew		I (Idho)	Knowledge of the ancestors (**Beware – yew is deadly poisonous**)

HEALING PROPERTIES OF TREES

Birch leaf tea

Make an infusion by steeping 5ml/1tsp of fresh or dried leaves in 1 cup boiling water. Sweeten with honey to make an aromatic tea for easing rheumatic pains or urinary infections.

Rowan berry liqueur

2 cups brandy, 2 cups sugar syrup (made with .5k/1lb/2 cups sugar and 2 cups water), 1 cup ripe rowan berries. Dry berries until shrivelled and then steep in brandy for 9 days. Boil the sugar syrup until it is to reduced to 1 cup. When cold, add the mixture to brandy. Mix 15ml/1 tbsp with a little cold water and use as a gargle for sore throats, or take a teaspoonful of neat liqueur to soothe inflamed tonsils.

Ash decoction

Place 50g/2oz of dried ash leaves in 2 cups of water, boil for five minutes, add honey to taste and then drink a sherry glass of the cooled decoction morning, noon and night to bring down a fever.

Alder salve
Crush fresh leaves; rub on chapped skin.

Willow bark tea
Make a decoction using 25g/1oz willow bark and 1 cup water. Sip half a cup to cure a headache.

Hawthorne lotion
At Beltane, shake hawthorn branches and collect the flowers on a cloth. Add 50g/1oz of hawthorn flowers to 2 cups water, boil for five minutes, bottle and use as a skin lotion to prevent acne.

Oak bark gargle
Make a decoction using 50g/2oz of oak bark to 2 cups water. Use as a gargle to cure mouth ulcers.

Holly cold cure
Add 50g/2oz finely chopped leaves to 4 cups water. Soak for 2 hours then boil for 10 minutes. Leave to infuse for another 15 minutes then add lots of honey to counteract the bitter taste. Sip a cup three times a day to drive off a cold.

Hazelnut cough remedy
Grind 50g/2oz nuts to a very fine powder, add 30ml/2tbsp honey and stir into a glass of white wine. Sip three times daily for relief.

Vine leaf styptic
Crush a leaf and apply to small cuts to stop the bleeding.

Ivy compress
Make a decoction of 100g/4oz fresh ivy leaves and 2 cups water. Soak a pad in the decoction while still warm and apply to bumps and sprains to reduce swelling.

Elderflower bardic tonic
Steep 15ml/1tbsp of freshly gathered elderflowers in a glass of white wine overnight. Sip throughout the day to keep your singing voice sweet.

Fir balsam
Simmer 100g/4oz fresh fir tips in 1 cup water. Use as an inhalant to clear the nose and chest.

Furze antiseptic
Steep a large handful of fresh, bruised furze (gorse) flowers in 1 cup whisky or vodka. Leave in a sealed jar for two weeks. Carefully strain, re-bottle and use on cuts and grazes.

Heather tea
Make up a mix (to your own taste) of heather tops, young blackberry leaves, wild thyme and wild strawberry leaves. Drink fresh or dried as a spring tonic.

Poplar salve
(NB this recipe uses black poplar, *populus nigra*)
Make a decoction of 250g/8oz/2 cups fresh poplar buds to 2 cups water. Add the decoction to .5kg/1lb/2 cups white fat (lard or vegetable lard) and simmer very gently until all the water has evaporated. Strain and bottle. Use to soothe cracked skin, inflammation and piles.

Restricted plants UK
These rare plants are completely protected by the law (in Britain)

Gentiana nivalis
Orchis militaris
Cicerbita alpina
Orchis simia
Woodsia alpina
Woodsia ilvensis
Phyllodoce caerulea
Cephalanthera rubra
Diapensia lapponica
Lloydia serotina
Saxifraga cernua
Veronica spicata
Epipogium aphyllum
Gentia verna
Trichomanes speciosum
Minuartia stricta
Cyprepedium calceolus
Saxifraga caespotisa
Daphne mezereum
Gladiolus illyricus
Dianthus gratianopolitanus

Amber

Green calcite

Citrine

CRYSTALS

Aventurine Dispels negativity while enhancing the positive. Calms emotional upheaval. Soothing and balancing.

Affinity with   Thymus gland

Colour   Green

Amber (fossilized resin)

     Amber forms a link between the world of plants and minerals. Protective, grounding and harmonizing, amber promotes physical, mental and spiritual health.

Affinity with   Endocrine system, spleen, heart and thyroid

Colour   Honey, through deep amber to brown

Amethyst Brings serenity and helps enhance intuitive and psychic abilities. Shields from negative energies and a sense of being overwhelmed. Known as the 'stone of contentment', it enhances honesty and good will.

Affinity with   Astrological sign Scorpio

Colour   Purple

Bloodstone Calms the mind and helps to detoxify the blood. Builds confidence and aids concentration and perception.

Affinity with   Heart, blood system, base of spine chakra, sexuality

Colour   Dark green/black with red blotches

Azurite 'The Jewel of Wisdom', Azurite aids meditation and helps the user contact their unconscious mind. It is said to revive the brain. Helps to release the past.

Affinity with   Thyroid, astrological sign Sagittarius

Colour   Blue

Calcite Crystal of perception, Calcite helps the user integrate new ideas and changes. Calcite is also useful for cleansing and meditation.

Affinity with   Liver, kidneys and bones

Colour   Clear/yellow/green

Carnelian Grounding, anchoring and focuses on the present. Enhances self-esteem and feelings of security and personal power.

Affinity with   The sexual organs (Carnelian is a well-known fertility symbol); astrological sign Leo

Colour   Red

Chrysoprase Promotes creativity, releases tension and lifts the spirits, benefits new projects.

Affinity with   Astrological signs Aquarius, Gemini and Cancer

Colour   Green

Citrine A stone of the sun, citrine enhances spiritual growth, personal power and intent. It is uplifting and energizing.

Affinity with   Astrological sign Virgo

Colour   Yellow

Emerald Powerful healing stone.

Affinity with   All organs of the body; astrological signs Cancer, Taurus and Libra

Colour   Clear green

Fluorite Increases spiritual awareness; it also enhances mental capabilities.

Affinity with   Teeth and bones; stimulates the heart chakra; astrological sign Pisces

Colour   Green/mauve/clear

Garnet	Calming, soothing, garnets encourage the flow of earth energy into the body.
Affinity with	Base of spine chakra, lower limbs, astrological sign Capricorn
Colour	Ruby red
Hematite	Protective and grounding, hematite helps form a connection with the earth and benefits astral projection. Promotes self-esteem and is thought to aid detoxification of the blood.
Affinity with	Blood system; 'true self'; astrological signs Virgo and Capricorn
Colour	Grey/silver
Lapis Lazuli	Reveals inner truth and helps the user achieve spiritual enlightenment and greater communication.
Affinity with	The immune system; astrological signs Taurus, Aquarius and Sagittarius
Colour	Deep intense blue
Moonstone	Creates emotional balance; its energies are soothing and healing. Moonstone is said to be feminine in nature and to have a positive effect on the menstrual cycle.
Affinity with	Astrological sign Gemini
Colour	Cream, through peach to grey
Obsidian	Obsidian is thought to act as a protector and to help us to face our true natures.
Affinity with	The eyes; astrological sign Scorpio
Colour	Glassy black
Pyrite (Fools' Gold)	
	Pyrite is said to help concentration, improve memory, and increase your ability to deal with complex issues. It is also said to act as a shield.
Affinity with	Blood system, all astrological signs
Colour	Gold
Quartz	Quartz strengthens all the positive aspects of the personality. It is a calming crystal that negates feelings of anger and fear.
Affinity with	All astrological signs, all parts of the body
Colour	Clear
Rose Quartz	Opens up the emotions, amplifies love, brings comfort and helps to heal emotional wounds.
Affinity with	Heart, circulatory system, astrological sign Cancer
Colour	Pale, clouded pink
Sodalite	Clears the mind and encourages rational thought.
Affinity with	Astrological sign Aquarius
Colour	Dark blue with white flecks
Topaz	Soothes, calms and aids relaxation. Topaz is said to illuminate your inner path.
Affinity with	Nervous system, astrological signs Aries, Leo and Gemini
Colour	Yellow

Faden Quartz

Fluorite

Lapis lazuli

HOW TO MAKE YOUR OWN ATHAME

It is possible (although very time consuming) to make your own athame blade even if you have no blacksmith's forge. Don't attempt this unless you have some knowledge of working with metal as, in some of the processes, the blade will become extremely hot.

First buy a piece of untempered steel (i.e. steel that can be tempered). To work this you will need a coarse and a fine steel file, a hacksaw with a blade tough enough to cut steel, and a barbecue.

Light a large fire in your barbecue early in the morning and, when all the coals are red-hot, carefully position your steel. Using tongs, make sure the steel is completely covered with hot coals. It should eventually become a dull red colour. You will now need to leave the steel in the barbecue for several hours. Leave your steel until the coals are quite cold. Remember, do not leave a fire unattended. If the steel is still too hard to work, repeat the process.

When the steel is cold, mark on it the shape of your double-edged blade. Remember to include a tang (this is the short point, which holds the blade into the hilt).

Using the hacksaw carefully, cut out the shape of your blade. Take great care when doing this, as the metal will be extremely jagged. Once you have your shape, file the edges down using the two different grades of file, until the blade outline is smooth. Finish the process with 'wet and dry' sandpaper until it is completely smooth.

Now you have to retemper the blade so it will remain hard.

Light your barbecue again and this time try to make sure the blade becomes a bright, rather than a dull, red. You may have to fan the barbecue to get the right amount of heat.

When the blade is bright red, use your tongs to lift it into a large bucket of very warm water. Always remember to take great care – you should wear gloves, a pair of protective goggles, and tongs with the longest handles you can find. Be careful when you place the blade into the bucket as the water may spit and boil.

Allow the steel to cool completely and then sand it down with 'wet and dry'. Repeat the heating process but, as in the first heating, only allow your blade to become dull red. It will then become pale yellow. Just after this stage is reached, the steel will dull to a warm yellow. Lift the blade into warm water again. When it is cold you can polish and sharpen your blade. Fit it into a hilt as described earlier.

Thanks to Hamish Miller for his kind advice on the forging process.

CORRESPONDENCES FOR FINGER MAGIC

Little finger	Air/earth
Ring finger	Water/fire
Middle finger	Fire/water
Forefinger	Earth/air
Thumbs	Spirit

Right little finger	Mercury
Right ring finger	Neptune
Right middle finger	Mars
Right forefinger	Saturn
Right thumb	Sun

Left thumb	Moon
Left forefinger	Jupiter
Left middle finger	Uranus
Left ring finger	Venus
Left little finger	Pluto

Below

The 'true witch's weapon', the athame is attuned to its owner and is one of the most personal tools.

CORRESPONDENCES FOR THE DAYS OF THE WEEK

DAY	PLANET	MAGICAL WORK	GEMS
Sunday	Sun	Contacting solar deities, healing, expansion, divine inspiration and spells connected with authority and friendships	topaz, gold
Monday	Moon	Contacting lunar deities, peace, intuition, synthesis, dream work, psychic growth, divination, enhancing spiritual awareness	moonstone, pearl
Tuesday	Mars	Magic connected with courage, passion, competition, conflict, vitality and strength	ruby, garnet, iron
Wednesday	Mercury	Contacting deities of intellect, Hermes, Thoth, Mercury, magic connected with communication, intellect, learning, study, wisdom and divination	amethyst, silver
Thursday	Jupiter	Connecting with father gods, Zeus, magic associated with expansion, generosity, money, prosperity, luck, loyalty	sapphire, gold
Friday	Venus	Contacting goddesses of love, magic concerning love, fertility, pleasure, creativity	emerald, copper
Saturday	Saturn	Contacting planet and god Saturn, magic connected with transformation, death/rebirth, mourning, wills, long life, endings	obsidian, diamond

PROPERTIES OF GUMS AND RESINS FOR INCENSE-MAKING

NAME	RULED BY	DEITIES	FESTIVALS	PROPERTIES
Benzoin	Mercury	Mercury	Air rites, all incenses	Clears the mind, cleansing, inspiration
Copal	Sun	Fire deities	Fire rites, all incenses	Cleansing,
Dammar	Mercury	Air deities	All incenses	Inspiration
Dragon's Blood	Mars	Athena, Minerva, deities of war	Fire rites, all incenses	Strength, lust, energy
Frankincense	Sun	Solar Gods	Solstices, fire rituals all rituals,	Consecration, purification, aids meditation
Mastic	Sun	Fire deities	Fire rituals	Purification
Myrrh	Moon	Isis, Hecate, Water/moon deities	All rituals, funerals, memorial services	Increases spiritual awareness
Oak Moss (oil)	Earth	Horned God	Horned God rituals, all rites	Grounding, energy, vitality
Pine resin (colophony)	Mars	Fire deities	Solar deities, all incenses	Growth, fertility, purification
Storax	Sun	Fire deities	Solar deities	Purification

Caledonii Tradition

A Wiccan tradition that concentrates on Scottish customs and lore.

Ceremonial Witchcraft

A branch of Wicca that explores elaborate ceremonial rituals from various sources. These might be Kabbalistic, Egyptian or Western in origin.

Dianic Wicca

Goddess-based Wicca, in which the God is largely ignored. Dianic Wicca is strongly feminist and advocates political activism.

Eclectic Wicca

Those who are eclectic witches do not subscribe to any one tradition but instead 'pick and mix' the strands which they find most useful.

Faery Tradition (Radical Faeries)

A gay male spiritual path, which borrows from Wicca, magic and other earth mysteries.

Gardnerian Wicca

Gerald Gardner did much in the early 1950s to popularize Wicca. His branch of 'skyclad' ritual, with an emphasis on the land and the seasonal cycle, has become one of the 'standard' forms of modern Wicca.

Hedge-witchcraft

A solo branch of witchcraft concentrating on the practical side of magic such as healing and spell-casting. Hedge-witches have a strong personal relationship with nature and are not affiliated to organizations or covens.

Hereditary Witchcraft

An ancient and somewhat secretive branch of Wicca in which a family, or group of families, will only train and initiate their own relatives.

BASIC ESBAT INCENSE

3 parts	Frankincense
1 part	Myrrh
1 part	Benzoin
9 drops	Pure rose oil
9 drops	Oakmoss oil
1 drop	Water
$1/4$ part	Oil-honey-wine mix

You can adapt this recipe for all your esbats/sabbats by adding appropriate oils, seeds, flowers and so on.

TYPES OF WICCA

Alexandrian

A modification of Gardnerian Wicca, Alexandrian Wicca developed out of the rituals of Alex Sanders in Britain in the 1960s.

Celtic Wicca

A tradition based on ancient Celtic lore, emphasizing the relationship with nature and the land. Practitioners venerate spirits of the land such as brownies, fairies, elves and gnomes.

Pictish Witchcraft

Similar to Caledonii Wicca in that it focuses on Scottish tradition and lore. Pictish or Petti-wicca emphasizes self-sufficiency and direct experience of the wild.

Seax-Wicca

Founded by Raymond Buckland, Saex-Wicca centres on personal encounters with nature and looks to Saxon lore for inspiration.

Stregeria

Italian witchcraft, based on the seminal text, *The Gospel of the Witches*.

Welsh Wicca

Welsh Wicca is based on the Welsh Celtic tradition and focusing on nature spirits and the land.

Useful Addresses

If you would like to learn more about Wicca or study groups on Wicca, you can contact me by sending a stamped, addressed envelope to:

Rowan Tree and Red Thread
PO Box 11, Rye
TN31 6WP, UK

EUROPE

The majority of the groups listed are staffed by volunteers, so please enclose a large stamped, addressed envelope or international reply coupons if you would like to hear from them.

Aradia Trust
BM Deosil,
London WC1N 3XX, UK
(Information on Wicca and study groups)

Cauldron Magazine,
M Howard
Caemorgan Cottage, Caemorgan Rd
Cardigan, Dyfed, Wales, SA43 1QU, UK

Children of Artemis,
BM Artemis,
London, WC1N 3XX, UK
Email: media@witchcraft.org
(Information on Wicca and study groups)

Circe
Postbus2191
3500 GD, Utrecht
The Netherlands

Circle du Dragon
BP 68, 33034 Bordeaux Cedex
France
Email: troisp@hol.fr

Marian Green
BCM Quest
London, WC1N 3XX, UK
(Runs a correspondence course on natural magic based on her books, and runs seminars and workshops in the UK and Europe)

Hoblink (Gay/bisexual pagan contacts)
Box 814
Southampton, SO17 2SZ, UK
(Quarterly newsletter: Box 22, OUT Brighton, 4–7 Dorset St, Brighton, BN2 1AW, UK)

Museum of Witchcraft
Graham King
Museum of Witchcraft, Boscastle
North Cornwall, PL35 0HD, UK
01840 250 111
Web site: museumofwitchcraft.com
(Largest display of Witchcraft artefacts in Britain, information on Wicca and witchcraft. Extensive library and archive available for research by appointment)

The Pagan Federation
The Secretary
BM Box 7097
London, WC1N 3XX, UK
Secretary@paganfed.demon.co.uk
(Information on paganism, Wicca, training groups and open rituals)

Other Pagan Groups

British Druid Order
P.O. Box 29
St Leonards-on-Sea
East Sussex, TN37 7YP, UK

Eco Magic
Dragon
23b Pepys Road
London, SE14 5SA, UK
Email: adrian@dragonnetwork.org
(Ecological magic to protect the earth)

Fellowship of Isis
Clonegal Castle, Enniscorthy
Wexford, Eire
(International Goddess-based organization)

London Earth Mysteries Circle
Rob Stephenson
PO Box 1035
London W2 6ZX, UK

Minor Arcana
P.O. Box 615
Norwich, Norfolk, NR1 4QQ, UK
(Free contact network for youngsters, with newsletter)

Odinshof
BM Tercel
London, WC1N 3XX, UK
(Teaching and other activities in the Northern/Norse tradition)

Order of Bards, Ovates and Druids
PO Box 1333
Lewes
East Sussex, BN7 1DX, UK
(Information and correspondence courses on Druidry)

Servants of the Light
P.O. Box 215
St Helier
Jersey, Channel Islands, JE4 9SD
(Western Mysteries school with correspondence courses – founded by a student of Dion Fortune: currently headed by Dolores Ashcroft Nowicki)

Secret Chiefs (previously Talking Stick)
P.O. Box 3719
London, SW17 8XT, UK
(Fortnightly discussion group every second Wednesday at the Princess Louise pub, High Holborn, London, 7.30pm for 8.30pm start)

USA and CANADA

Church of All Worlds
PO Box 488
Laytonville
California 95454, USA
(Pagan information, magazine Green Egg*)*

Circle
P.O. Box 219, Mount Horeb
WI 53572, USA
(Publishes Circle Network News *and* Circle Guide to Pagan Groups, *gatherings, information on paganism)*

Hecate's Loom
Box 5206
Station B, Victoria, BC
V8R 6N4, Canada
Email: loom@island-net.com
(Wiccan information and gatherings)

The Pagan Federation
c/o Michael Thorn
P.O. Box 408
Shirley, NY 11967-0408, USA

Reclaiming
P.O. Box 14404
San Francisco
CA 94114, USA
(Goddess-based workshops, gatherings
and open rituals affiliated with
Starhawk)

Wiccan Church of Canada
109 Vaughan Road
Toronto, M6C2L9
Canada

AUSTRALIA AND NEW ZEALAND

GRAIL Directory
G.P.O. Box 1444
Canberra City 2601, ACT
Australia
(Useful resource for finding groups,
gatherings and open rituals)

Pan Pacific Pagan Alliance
P.O. Box 823
Bathurst, NSW 2795
Australia
http://www.summit.net.au/pppa/
(information on Wicca and paganism
across Australia)

Pagan Alliance (NZ)
P.A.N.Z.
P O Box 33
Petone, Wellington
New Zealand

SUPPLIERS
INCENSE

alexander-essentials.com
Offers a great range of oils with
information about each product.
They also stock some censers

www.baldwins.co.uk
G. Baldwins & Co
Freepost LON7690
London, SE17 1BR, UK
Tel: 020 7703 5550
Excellent selection of resins, dried
herbs and essential oils

incensemagic.co.uk
Oils, resins and mixers

www.panspantry.co.uk
Good selection of oils and incense
ingredients

somethingforthewickend.com
Good selection of candles and wide
range of essential oils

GENERAL

http://www.hermeticka.com
Officially ritual magic rather than
witchcraft supplies, but a good source
of tools and altar cloths

http://www.mesmerize-uk.com
26 Wellgate
Rotherham, South Yorkshire
S60 2LR, UK
Large selection statues, tarot cards,
crystals, books and witchcraft supplies

http://www.newmoon.uk.com
P.O. Box 110
Didcot, Oxon
OX11 9YT, UK
Large selection of mail order
witchcraft supplies including Egyptian
jewellery and statues, crystals, Celtic
designs, ritual tools and crystal balls

http://www.rowanmoon.com
Pagan equipment, jewellery and tools

Seven Veils
59 Wickham Avenue
North Cheam, Sutton, Surrey
SM3 8DX, UK
Excellent-value robes and cloaks
made to your specifications

http://www.spiral.org.uk
173 High Street
Rochester, Kent
ME1 1EH, UK
(+44) 01634 401 274
Large variety of pagan supplies,
historical reproductions, cards,
pendants, swords and athames

www.triplemooninc.com
15 Rowdehouse Circle
Needham, Massachusetts, 02492
USA
Good email team and excellent choice
of natural wood athames, ritual tools,
altar cloths and spell supplies

http://www.witchware.com
Huge web site featuring jewellery,
incenses, tools etc

http://www.wyrdshop.com
154 Cannongate
Edinburgh, EH8 8DD, UK
Excellent and massive choice of
witchcraft supplies, tools, statues, tarot
sets and jewellery. Beautiful chalices,
cauldrons and runes

paganjewellery.com
(Caduceus' on line shop.) Celtic,
Gothic and Egyptian jewellery

www.spiritoftheforest.co.uk
Beautiful hand-carved wooden
pendants, brooches and earrings

Index